Forgiving Our Limitations

THE PRACTICE OF *A COURSE IN MIRACLES*

THE HEALING POWER OF KINDNESS

Volume Two

Forgiving Our Limitations

KENNETH WAPNICK, Ph.D.

Foundation for A COURSE IN MIRACLES®

Foundation for A Course in Miracles®
41397 Buecking Drive
Temecula, CA 92590
www.facim.org

First printing, 2005
Second printing, 2009

Printed in the United States of America

Portions of *A Course in Miracles* copyright 1975, 1992
Psychotherapy: Purpose, Process and Practice copyright 1976, 1992
The Song of Prayer copyright 1976, 1992
The Gifts of God copyright 1982
by the *Foundation for A Course in Miracles*®

Library of Congress Cataloging-in-Publication Data

Wapnick, Kenneth
   The healing power of kindness / Kenneth Wapnick.
   p.   cm.
   Includes index.
   ISBN 978-1-59142-155-1 (v. 2)
   1. Course in miracles. 2. Kindness--Religious aspects. 3. Spiritual life--New Age movement. I. Title.
   BP605.C68W3535 2005
   299'.93--dc22   2005002869

CONTENTS

Preface

This book is based on two workshops given at the Foundation: "Shadows of Limitation" and "Sweet Are the Uses of Adversity."* The transcripts have been edited to enhance readability; yet, as with all the books in this series on the practice of *A Course in Miracles*, their relative informality has been retained. Some questions from the workshops have been incorporated into the general discussion, and new material has been added to elaborate on certain points. As with *Releasing Judgment*—Volume One of *The Healing Power of Kindness*—it is my hope that the present book will encourage students of *A Course in Miracles* to be kinder and gentler with themselves and others. In so doing, we walk the kind path that heals our minds and leads us home.

I should like to thank our Director of Publications, Rosemarie LoSasso, for continuing to be such a faithful shepherd of my books in her role as editor. This latest is but another witness to her many wonderful years of conscientious dedication to *A Course in Miracles* and to the Foundation's work.

---

* The workshops were presented in September 2003 and September 2004, and are available on CD.

Preface

Introduction

The theme of this book derives from one sentence in the text and one in the manual for teachers:

> Concentrate only on this [the little willingness], and be not disturbed that shadows surround it. That is why you came (T-18.IV.2:4-5).

> Do not despair, then, because of limitations. It is your function to escape from them, but not to be without them (M-26.4:1-2).

Both sentences share a basic content or meaning, but their focus differs. The former centers on the idea of shadows, specifically Jesus' loving directive that we be not disturbed by their presence in ourselves; the latter centers on the idea of limitations, and Jesus' loving directive that we not despair over them. The first statement, however, relates to our being in the classroom that is the world, so we may learn; the second, so we may teach. Yet, Jesus emphasizes that teaching and learning are the same, and the opening page of the manual states: "To teach is to demonstrate" (M-in.2:1). However, we cannot demonstrate what we have not learned; and once we learn, we inevitably teach. Unlike what the world believes, *A Course in Miracles* views both teaching and learning as irrelevant to the body or brain, involving only

1

our state of mind. Since the mind of God's Son is one, what we learn we learn for everyone, and what we teach we teach everyone.

Though teaching and learning are the same, their emphasis differs, and this will be reflected in our discussion. We begin by talking about what it means to be in this world as a classroom in which we learn the Holy Spirit's lessons of forgiveness, and conclude by discussing our role as instruments through which the Holy Spirit teaches. Throughout, the unifying theme will be the ego's shadows of limitation that constitute our collective and personal thought systems, these shadows becoming transformed from the ego's instruments of damnation to the Holy Spirit's means of salvation.

1. Shadows of Limitations: Limiting the Limitless

We cannot really talk about the limited without first having understood what it is a reaction against, and so we begin with a discussion of limitlessness. God is perfect Love and Oneness, an infinite Being of Wholeness and Totality. No limitation exists in Him, which means there is no separation, differentiation, or distinction—only perfect Love. The nature of reality, therefore, is limitless, there being no place, as the workbook says, where the Father ends and the Son begins as something apart from Him (W-pI.132.12:4). However, once there is separation there is limitation, for separation limits the limitless. For instance, there are limits in my relationship with you because we are separate—separate personalities inhabiting separate bodies; moreover, needs are built-in limitations, accentuating our differences with each other.

In other words, being born into this physical world is a limitation. Contrary to the ego's first law of chaos that there is a hierarchy of illusions (T-23.II.2:3), the Holy Spirit's thought system rests on the principle that there is no hierarchy of illusions and therefore no hierarchy of limitations. Thus, an illusion is an illusion is an illusion; a limitation is a limitation is a limitation. Whether large or small, everything here remains a limitation.

In addition, all limitations are purposive. Whether the limitations are major or minor, they remain integral to the ego's purpose of replacing limitless reality with separation in the form of a world of individual beings, limited by their very nature. Jesus reveals this ultimate purpose of bodies in the ego's strategy:

> It is only the awareness of the body that makes love seem limited. For the body *is* a limit on love. The belief in limited love was its origin, and *it was made to limit the unlimited*. Think not that this is merely allegorical, for it was made to limit *you* (T-18.VIII.1:1-4; italics mine in 1:3).

A major objective of *A Course in Miracles* is to teach us the importance of *purpose*, and in the above passage Jesus presents a statement of purpose by saying that the body was made to limit the unlimited. Jesus was telling Helen, and all of us: "I am not speaking in allegory, symbols, or metaphor here, but telling you very specifically that the body was made to limit the unlimited." Since the unlimited is love, the body was made to limit love. Yet can the body's purpose be changed:

> Made to be fearful, must the body serve the purpose given it. But we can change the purpose that the body will obey by changing what we think that it is for (W-pII.5.3:4-5).

The thought of limitation originates in the mind, and since *ideas leave not their source*—a central principle in *A Course in Miracles*—the mind is where the thought remains. There is nothing other than mind, but the body's purpose is to make the thought of limitation reality. By its very nature, a body limits—to wit, two bodies cannot occupy the same space at the same time, representing in form the underlying content of limitation. This intent to limit by emphasizing the ego's separation and specialness can be identified in some fairly common experiences in our daily lives. Grandparents, for example, often say about their grandchildren, especially when they are young and there is still the pretense of their being loving and innocent: "You are so adorable and sweet I want to eat you up!" This feeling also emerges when one person falls in love with another. You want to cannibalize the beloved, to have that innocence and sweetness inside *you*, which is exactly what we believe we did with God when we sought to cannibalize His Love, creative power, and life, making them our own. And so Jesus says the body was made as a limit on love, and the limiting was made to limit the limitless—the ego's underlying purpose.

In a message to Helen that was a prelude to *The Song of Prayer,* Jesus gently chided his scribe for asking him for specific help. He said to her that in so asking him she was trying to manage the unmanageable.* He could just as easily have said she was trying to limit the unlimited—his love. Love is frightening because it is all-encompassing, and within it there is no room for specialness or individual uniqueness. Therefore, everything we made to define ourselves becomes meaningless in love's presence, and in response to that threat, we attempt to limit love by making it be like us—the meaning of being limited and specific.

Our eagerness to go to the Holy Spirit with our specific requests led Jesus to dictate *The Song of Prayer*. He told Helen, and all of us, that in asking for specific help we attempt to take his limitless love— mirroring the love of our Self—and limit it, seeking to put a frame around his love so we can manage and control it. We express our fear by asking for specific help, telling him we do not want to experience his love, but instead want him to tell us where to go to buy something, how to get a job, or what to do so that our bodies will be healed of disease. We want all this in order to maintain our limited selves, accomplished by bringing his unlimited self to our limitation.

---

* See *Absence from Felicity: The Story of Helen Schucman and Her Scribing of A COURSE IN MIRACLES*, p. 445.

This accounts for the guilt and conflict associated with a relationship with Jesus. On some level we know we are trying to replicate and re-enact what we originally did with our Creator—attempting to manage Jesus by bringing his limitless love into our limited illusion, as seen in the attempts throughout the ages of people making God into something tangible and corporeal—a Person Who is specifically there for them.

Whenever you are tempted to call attention to what you think is a limitation, deficiency, or defect, something that leaves you poor in comparison to someone else's wealth (finances, abilities, beauty, youth, or innocence), be aware that you but strive to make the limitation into a reality in which there is pain, suffering, loss, and sacrifice—some lose, others gain. "The rock on which salvation rests," Jesus tells us, is the "rebirth of the idea no one can lose for anyone to gain" (T-25.VII.12:7,1), correcting the ego's idea of salvation, which is that for one to win, another must lose—*one or the other.* This ego principle becomes an inherent part of the separated Son's nature. The Sonship becomes limited—no longer total, universal, or unified—but divisible into categories and camps: the successful and the unsuccessful, the good and the bad, those with abilities and those without them.

To the ego, our bodies serve a most important purpose: proving that limited love is the reality; indeed, that limitation *is* reality—which is another way of saying separation is reality. I emphasize this point because of the temptation, to which we almost always succumb, to focus on specific limitations. In doing so, we validate the ego's first law of chaos that there is a hierarchy of illusions. Instead, we should remember that simply being in a body is a limitation, a shadow of the *thought* of limitation. We are not in touch with this thought because we are not in touch with the mind, being aware only of the physical and psychological experience directly associated with being a body.

Yet what we do with the body tells us what we believe we have done with the mind. Anything the body does that separates, limits, judges, or seeks specialness tells us we have chosen the thought system of separation, limitation, judgment, and specialness— the thought system of the ego. All we need do to find out which teacher we have chosen—the Holy Spirit or the ego—is to pay attention to what our bodies appear to be doing. I use the word *appear*, because the body really does nothing. It is the mind that "does" by its choice, which it acts out through the body—the mind's projection. The problem is never the body or its limitations, but what we *do* with these limitations. That is why, when we become disturbed or upset by limitations—what Jesus cautions us about in the two statements quoted above—we do exactly what the

ego wants by rooting our attention in the mindless—
the body—so we will never return to where the problem of limitation truly is—the mind's decision. We
can thus say that Jesus' purpose in *A Course in
Miracles* is to make us mind*ful* rather than mind*less*.
The ego took its original thought of limitation in the
mind and protected it through projection, making up a
limited world with limited bodies. This dynamic
causes us to forget that we—as decision-making
minds—literally made up the world. We are aware
now only of our experience as a limited, imperfect
body in a limited, imperfect world, with no memory
of how we got there.

To attempt to make the body better or perfect is the
same mistake as trying to make the world better or
perfect, for they were made to make the perfect imperfect and to limit the limitless. Therefore, unless
you change the *source* of the world—the mind's decision to identify with the ego rather than the Holy
Spirit—nothing you do to improve it or the body will
work, at least not permanently, for you will not have
undone the imperfect and limited guilt that is the
source of the imperfection and limitation. Again, the
purpose of *A Course in Miracles* is to return us to the
source of the limitation so we can make a different
choice; i.e., choose the Voice that speaks for the
unlimited, rather than continually choose and identify
with the voice that speaks for the limited.

When we seek to change the body or the world, we do precisely what the ego wants. Why would I try to fix my body or the world unless I believed there were something that needed fixing? A world of imperfection and limitation reflects the underlying *thought* of imperfection and limitation—which, needless to say, is wonderful for the ego because what is imperfect is perfect in its warped sight. Not only does the world reflect this imperfection, but it protects it. Having forgotten we made the world, we are aware only of a world that is seen as independent of the mind. We all have been taught, believe and experience—consciously or not—that we were born into a world that preceded us and will succeed us after we die. None of that is true. We—the decision-making part of our minds—made the world, which has never left its source in the collective mind.

As we will see repeatedly, if we do not change the world's underlying purpose and instead attempt to change the shadow, we will end up simply substituting one shadow for another; and then the shadow's source—the mind's decision to remain imperfect and limited—will remain intact. We read in the text about the mistake inherent in making the body real and an object for our judgments:

> The thing you hate and fear and loathe and want, the body does not know. You send it forth to

seek for separation and be separate. And then you hate it, not for what it is, but for the uses you have made of it. You shrink from what it sees and what it hears, and hate its frailty and littleness. And you despise its acts, but not your own. It sees and acts for *you*. It hears your voice. And it is frail and little by your wish. It seems to punish you, and thus deserve your hatred for the limitations that it brings to you. Yet you have made of it a symbol for the limitations that you want your mind to have and see and keep (T-28.VI.3).

Jesus' intention, consequently, is to help us understand that external limitations can serve a different purpose if we place them in his hands. The ego's purpose for the limited and imperfect world and body is to keep us from returning to the mind. Jesus' purpose is to teach us how to use the world and body so they direct us to the mind, where we can then choose the Voice that speaks for limitlessness instead of limitation—again, the shift from *mindlessness* to *mindfulness*. That is the importance of his caution: "Be not disturbed that shadows surround it. That is why you came." When you become upset with the shadows—your faults, deficiencies, illnesses, past abuse and victimization—you but make the shadows real.

Asking Jesus for help means—and in his course it is the *only* thing it means—that he help you recognize that what you relate to is a shadow. People in their right minds do not change a shadow, because they realize it is nothing. If you walk outside and see a shadow, you know it has no substance in and of itself, for its nothingness is the absence of light. Stated another way, the mind's shadows are present because we chose against the Holy Spirit's light, and Jesus helps us realize that everything that troubles, disturbs, or upsets us—whether in the world at large or our personal world—is a shadow of a decision to remove ourselves from the light. Therefore, what has to be changed is the decision, not the shadow.

Plato taught this twenty-five hundred years ago; the world did not accept it then, and has not accepted it still. *A Course in Miracles* is a modern form of Platonism that teaches the difference between shadows and truth, appearance and reality. In the Master's well-known Allegory of the Cave, the prisoners in the cave's interior are chained so they can see only the back wall. Behind them is the mouth of the cave, which they cannot see because their attention has been riveted to the interior wall. Outside the cave's opening, the sun shines from behind those who pass back and forth along the road. The prisoners, however, see only the shadows of those passers-by on the wall in front of them. Since they cannot turn around, they believe that what they see is reality. Jesus' message, extending Plato's, is that we not be disturbed by the shadows, for that would give them a power, strength, and reality they do not have.

Whenever we get upset by anything in the world, we but allow ourselves to be disturbed by shadows. It does not matter whether we are upset by something perceived as major or minor—our favorite stock lost half a point, a loved one has cancer, or our baseball team lost. If our peace is shattered, disturbed, or threatened in any way, we are doing the ego's bidding of being disturbed by shadows.

The body was made to be extraordinarily sensitive to all kinds of stimuli—physical and psychological—and we react to them all, responding to shadows as if they were real. Although the body may react appropriately to what goes on around and within it, when you join Jesus in the mind above the battleground and look down, you realize that the body itself is a shadow, reacting to other shadows, an illusion reacting to illusions—all of which means that nothing is happening. When Jesus rhetorically asks in the Course whether thoughts are dangerous, his answer is: "To bodies, yes!" (T-21.VIII.1:1). As long as I identify with my body, what goes on around me—what others think and do—certainly has an effect on me. The limitations of others reinforce my own—another's body, already a limited expression of the ego, affects mine, also a limited expression. The problem is not the form the shadows of limitations take, but the mind's decision to be with the ego instead of the Holy Spirit, identifying with the idea of limited love instead of awakening to the reality of unlimited love.

It is essential when you are tempted to be upset by anything, to call to mind the thought that you should not be upset by the specific. You *should* be upset, though, by the fact you are here, or think you are here, for that is the original limitation that represents the mind's choosing to exist in a nightmare of limitation rather than awaken to limitlessness. Being upset about being here at least focuses our attention on the mind— our decision maker's power to choose. And that we can do something about.

As stated above, a positive aspect of our limitations is that they can be used to return us from *mindlessness* to *mindfulness*. When we are mindful— identifying with the mind as everything—we return to the decision maker that sees the terrible effects of choosing to live with limitation, when it could just as easily have chosen limitlessness. However, we must see clearly that our state of mind—how we experience the world—directly follows from the mind's decision. We made the body to be imperfect, sicken, and fail; we made the world to be imperfect and fail; we made relationships, governmental leaders, machines, and even weather patterns to fail. Indeed, we made everything to fail, which is what induces us to believe that the problem is external and demands attention and solution. From the beginning of what we think of as life to the present day, we have tried to make the imperfect perfect, the horrible beautiful, and the limited limitless—and we have failed abysmally. This is why the world is in no better shape today than it was twenty-five hundred years ago, twenty-five thousand years ago, or twenty-five million years ago. The forms of the shadows change, but their source remains constant, and will always remain constant until we return to the mind and make another choice.

Epictetus, the influential Greek philosopher who lived in the first century in Rome, was a member of the philosophical school of Stoicism that was founded around the turn of the fourth century B.C. by Zeno*. If you read Epictetus in light of *A Course in Miracles*, you will be astounded by his wisdom. His version of Stoicism taught that there is nothing you can do to change the world, but you can change how you react to it. Some of the Greek philosophers—Democritus, for instance—taught that the world consisted of atoms, which originally trickled through the universe, known as the void. The ultimate expression of these falling atoms was the physical universe that we know—specifically, our individual lives in bodies.

---

* Zeno taught in the *stoa poikile* (painted Colonnade) in Athens; accordingly, his adherents came to be known as Stoics.

Nothing could be done about how these atoms fell. That was a given, nature being the result of fortuitous combinations of atoms, with no ordering principle. Epictetus thus taught that the world is simply what it is, and the wise accept their roles within it, knowing there is no cause for either exultation or depression, for one position in life is no better or worse than another. A famous story of Epictetus, who was a slave, well illustrates this point. Enduring his leg being broken by his master, he said, matter-of-factly: "I warned you that my leg would break if you twisted too hard." And that was that.

Consequently, if, someone were to steal something from you, most likely you would not get it back, a situation over which you have no control. Yet you do have control over how you perceive the situation and how you react. Epictetus spoke of living a virtuous life, which meant a life of moderation. In fact, "moderation in all things" was the prevailing Greek motto. You do not allow yourself to become overly happy or sad, because one is the opposite side of the other. You recognize that the only meaning of anything here lies in its relationship to a life of virtue— one's inner life, over which you do have control. This was Epictetus' major point—our control over how we react to the world, which provides us with freedom even when we typically have no control over what goes on around us.

Epictetus did not say this, but *A Course in Miracles* certainly does: terrible things will happen because the world came from a terrible thought—"The world was made as an attack on God" (W-pII.3.2:1). It would have to be this way, since the world came from the thought of separation that said: "Limitless love and perfection are not enough; I want something more— the love and individual attention that God does not provide." In other words, we wanted specialness instead of love, separation instead of oneness. Telling God that His Love was not sufficient was therefore the original attack.

Since *ideas leave not their source*, the physical world of limitation, which we have already seen is a limit on love, has never left its source in the mind, wherein resides the original ego thought of limited love. Thus the world must be the terrible place that is the shadow of the ego's terrible thought. And so Jesus urges us not to be disturbed by the shadows, for if we are, it is only because we believe the shadows of our limitations and/or the world's limitations imprison us—they have a deleterious effect on our well being, for they can hurt us, prevent us from doing what we want, or make us do something against our will. At that point, the ego's perception of the body and world is perfectly reasonable and logical.

On the other hand, if we let ourselves be taught by our new teacher that the body and the world are simply symptoms, shadows, or projections of a decision for the limited thought that we are an ego—the real problem—our world and life will change. We will then perceive everything as a classroom in which we learn the only lesson right-minded people came to learn: limitations are the projections of a decision to be a limited self instead of the unlimited Self that God created. The world does not change, nor do the imperfections, defects, and deficiencies of the body. What changes are our perceptions. Remember that in *A Course in Miracles* perception is interpretation; not what the eyes physically see and report to the brain, but our reaction to what we see—having first looked through the eyes of the ego or the Holy Spirit.

The ego's eyes have you make the shadows real by becoming upset, disturbed, despairing, or ecstatic—especially when you see limitations in others instead of yourself. If the eyes are Jesus', however, you see everything as a classroom that will help you, and you are grateful because you realize that whatever happens can be transformed into a means of returning you to the decision for limitation in your mind. All things, without exception—a small bruise or cancer, a major or minor handicap—are seen as the same, because they remain a limitation coming from the mind's decision to be with the ego instead of the Holy Spirit. This is the willingness Jesus refers to in the passage about shadows, here in its fuller form:

> Trust not your good intentions. They are not
> enough. But trust implicitly your willingness,
> whatever else may enter. Concentrate only on this,
> and be not disturbed that shadows surround it.
> That is why you came. If you could come without
> them you would not need the holy instant
> (T-18.IV.2:1-6).

The well-intentioned always come from their egos
—wanting to help people and do good things they
consider significant and holy. That is why Jesus
teaches that "well-intentioned" in that sense is not the
issue. The willingness he asks us to trust implicitly relates to our decision to learn from him rather than the
ego. *This* is the issue, and not what we think we
should do to help ourselves or others. Accordingly, it
is not our reading and studying *A Course in Miracles*
that is important, but our little willingness to learn
what we are reading and studying, asking Jesus to
help us put his teachings into practice. This means
that the decision-making part of our minds has the
little willingness to begin questioning the limited outside and inside worlds the ego told us is reality. If we
could come without shadows, Jesus is saying, we
would not need the holy instant, the miracle, forgiveness, *A Course in Miracles*, nor him as our teacher. He
obviously speaks to our right-minded purpose when
he says "this is why you came"—the little willingness
to learn a different lesson from a different teacher.

This means, then, that our shadows, imperfections, and failures—physical and psychological—become part of the curriculum, the textbook Jesus uses to teach us how to look differently at these limitations. This "looking differently" is the meaning of forgiveness. Our becoming disturbed or excited by them means we have made them real, and have already chosen the ego as our teacher. We choose Jesus one minute, and the next change our minds because he teaches that our limitations are only shadows, as is the special self with which we identify. Our disturbance or obsession flies in his face and his teaching, which would never justify these reactions to ourselves or others. The ego naturally encourages and reinforces the decision to be affected by the shadows, withdrawing our little willingness. We thus say to the ego, "I prefer you and your teaching," reminiscent of what we did at the beginning when we said to God: "I don't like the way You do things, nor Your kind of love, and so I will make a different kind." At that point we replaced God and placed ourselves on creation's throne. The resultant self is the ego—our new creator, or, as the early pages of the text say, our *mis*creator.

Replacing Jesus as our teacher reflects the ontological replacement when we left God and His Love. That is why there is so much guilt associated with Jesus or the Holy Spirit. What we do to Them *is* what we believed we did to God. Whenever you allow yourself—and I use those words deliberately—to be upset by anything in this world, personal or collective, you have left Jesus. However, as soon as you become aware that something in the world has upset you and you ask for help, you return to him. The shadows your ego used to condemn you or others then become the curriculum Jesus uses to teach that the limitation is only in the mind—and *that* we can do something about. "The Special Function," which we will consider later, says that what we made to hurt or harm, the Holy Spirit uses to heal (T-25.VI.4:1). The limited body and defective personality we made to prove to God that we were not the ones who chose limitations —someone else did—become the curriculum when we ask Jesus for help. Those limitations, therefore, are the very means he uses to teach us that what is limited is not our personality, body, or ability, but the self we chose to replace the Self of Christ. Each and every time we are tempted to make the error of limitation real, he gently brings us back to the mind that made it, helping us understand why we did so.

We continually compensate for this original limitation of a self, over which we feel so guilty, because we used it as an attack on God. We secretly accuse ourselves of this sin of misusing the power of our minds. Everyone does this because we did it as one mind. The overpowering sense of guilt and wrongdoing we share comes from the thought: I took the power of my mind, and rather than have it be part of God's all-powerful Mind, I used it to separate from Him, thereby rendering His Mind ineffective, impotent, and non-existent because one Mind cannot be divided and continue to be. The guilt stemming from the mind's misuse is so enormous—having made a limited self not only to replace the unlimited but to attack it—all we can do is cope as best we can by projecting out a body, self, and world of limitation, but retain no responsibility for it.

During part of her career, Helen Schucman worked with retarded children, her professional love. Early in the scribing of *A Course in Miracles*, Jesus spoke with her about those who were born mentally retarded, as a way of helping her understand what he was teaching in the Course. He said these individuals chose retardation because they were trying to retard an overly-strong will, meaning that these entities accused themselves of having such a powerful and sinful mind that they would inevitably use it to destroy. They made their error real, and then compensated for it by making a self that was severely limited—what we call mental retardation. That is the reason no one ever truly understands the root cause of retardation, or any mental or physical illness. Researchers look for something external that is defective: a gene, chemical imbalance, environmental factors, or parental relationships—anything that is defective *except* the decision the mind has made. Only there can the defect be found and corrected. The same would hold for any mental or physical limitation, which can serve to prevent the sinful misuse of the mind's power. Those who so choose become innocent and powerless victims, defending against the accusation that they are *all*-powerful, and so protect themselves and others from their underlying tendency to kill, steal, cannibalize, rape, or abuse. The self they made is purposely limited, rendering their sinful minds totally inaccessible to misuse.

This, then, was Jesus' larger point to Helen. We come into the world with deficiencies and limitations, which are purposive, for they say to God: "Don't accuse me of being the aggressor, sinner, or murderer. Look—I am weak, limited, and powerless. How could I possibly steal from you or rape Your Love? Indeed, how could I destroy Heaven? Look at me—I cannot add up two and two correctly, or read words on this page; I cannot tie my own shoelaces, drive a car, hold down a job, or sustain a satisfactory relationship." Thus we all have things we cannot do, or cannot do correctly. Purpose is everything, and our purpose, once again, is to establish that the limitation is real as well as its underlying thought, but we are not responsible for it.

Consequently, when we become upset over limitations, we freeze the process of healing and make it impossible to return to the mind, whether the judgment is with our limitations or those of others. As long as we see the problem as in the body—mine or another's, my world or the world at large—we tell Jesus we are not interested in his lesson, for the ego's lesson that the world of limitations is real is far more attractive to us—not a shadow but reality—and presents a problem *not* in us that calls for action.

We need to recognize that we have made our limited worlds and defective bodies into prisons to demonstrate our innocence of the sins we lay on others. However, running from the power of the mind is a poor way to deal with the problem, and Jesus was certainly not suggesting to Helen that it was a good one. Solving the problem this way merely makes the error real: I have sinned; the sin is real; and now I ensure that I will never abuse that power again by living in a body that is defective, deficient, and disabled. It would be much more helpful, Jesus reminds us, for the mind to realize: I simply made a mistake, no different from the mistake everyone else has made, and there is a better way of correcting it. For example, the individual might come into the world with a powerful mind—we all have powerful minds—but experience its ability and intelligence. The opportunity is then taken to learn not to misuse the mind—it can be used to help rather than attack, abuse, or take advantage of others. This would be a right-minded way of handling the problem, for the limitation will have become a happy classroom of learning, rather than a prison of suffering.

In summary, we can generalize from Jesus' example of mental retardation to *all* circumstances in which people find themselves. In other words, our current physical and psychological states are chosen by the mind to achieve a purpose. Since the mind is split, this purpose is twofold: the wrong-minded ego wishes to maintain the belief in the reality of the sinful thought of separation by keeping the Son of God *mindless*, while the right-minded Holy Spirit corrects this by restoring to the Son awareness of his mind, teaching him to be *mindful* as he goes through his day, bringing his bodily experiences and reactions to the mind that is their source. Following the thought system of our new Teacher, we move past judging the *form* the body has taken to the mind's underlying *content*.

A Course in Miracles thus helps us understand—a step beyond Epictetus—that having made the world to keep us mindless, we can use it to return to the mind and our decision for the imperfect thought. We cannot change the world, but why would we want to? Why would we want to fool around with shadows, when we can change the shadow's *source*—the decision to be separated from the light. To paraphrase the Introduction to the text, this is not a course on love or light, but on removing the blocks to our awareness of the love and light (T-in.1:6-7). The original block to this awareness is the decision for limitation rather than limitlessness. We now see the world of limitation and shadows as an opportunity to return to our decision for the limited instead of the unlimited. This is the sum and substance of *A Course in Miracles*: to provide us with a Teacher Who helps us look at our limitations without judgment.

The Relinquishment of Judgment

The relinquishment of judgment is a key theme in *A Course in Miracles*. Indeed, one can say that this encapsulates the Holy Spirit's thought system. That is why it is necessary to recognize that whenever we emphasize our limitations, or seek to deny our own limitation by pointing out someone else's, we are judging. Anything that separates the Sonship by making the superficial differences among the Sonship important and real—and so deserving of judgment—reinforces the ego and prevents our ever leaving it. Comparison is inevitably involved in such a process, as the intention in comparing is to accentuate limitations: we commonly think someone else is smarter or more proficient, prettier or more handsome, a better athlete or student, and on and on. Whenever we compare ourselves to another—as superior or inferior—we say the Love of God is not One, mimicking the original judgment made against God and His Son.

Comparisons limit the unlimited, and thus Jesus tells us twice that "love makes no comparisons" (T-24.II.1:1; W-pI.195.4:2). They reinforce not only the illusion of our separation from each other—and from God—but the concept of limitations itself. When we compare, we elevate one and denigrate the other—the hallmark of the special love relationship: I love certain people because they are better than others, in the sense of being better for me. They meet my special needs, and therefore I love them for their special ability to love me rather than someone else. Moreover, comparisons implicitly involve a sense of what life would be like without limitations, defects, or deficiencies: I have a concept in my mind that I should be something other than I am. Inevitably involved in that judgment is the attack thought: someone or something made me this way. Whether my parents, genes, the world, or God—some external agent is responsible for my present state.

There is an inherent judgment in these perceptions of limitation because the original limitation was a judgment, our saying to God: "Your limitlessness and perfect Love are not enough for me. Consequently, I will leave your world and make my own." The world, therefore, has to be imperfect, for it is not of God, and thus not limitless or loving. When people experience love here, it is based upon externals—the ego's version of love. The same is true of the experience of liberation from the body's fetters, or whatever is believed to shackle it. That feeling is also illusory because it is based on the external. The true freedom of unlimited love is in the mind, having nothing to do with the body or the world.

We cannot make this happen by changing externals, but only by returning to what is within. "If *you* are not responsible for my deficiencies and defects, who is?" That, of course, is the question we never want to address. If the world did not make us into this egregious failure, the sorry specimen of homo sapiens we believe ourselves to be, then *we* did. This *we*, of course, is not the body—the ego's "hero" of the dream (T-27.VIII)—but the mind that chose this. *A Course in Miracles* helps us understand that the ego speaks first, is always wrong, and the Holy Spirit is the Answer (T-5.VI.3-4). We made ourselves to be imperfect, defective, and limited so that we can point an accusing finger at someone—anyone—and say: "You did this to me. Behold me, brother, at your hands I am imperfect, limited, and a failure. It is not my fault." In doing so we hope to get away with murder—literally—because murder is the source of our original belief in limitation. We believe that we—as one Son—killed God and destroyed Heaven. We cannibalized what was not ours—the creative power that gives eternal life, establishes a universe of spirit, and loves perfectly—believing we could make it our own. We seized all that at God's expense, which is the original thought of sin wherein our guilt is lodged.

We try to become free of that guilt, not by realizing nothing happened—which is what Jesus wants us to understand—but by making a world of bodies onto which we can project our guilt, which enables us to declare: "I am not the one who caused limitation. *You* did, and I am the limited, imperfect, failing proof of your misdeed." All this nicely serves the ego's purpose of keeping out of awareness the fact that we did this to ourselves. As long as we point an accusing finger at others, we can justifiably proclaim our innocence, and our limitations and handicaps witness that the ego thought system is alive and well, but not our responsibility. We fixate on and obsess about limitations, handicaps, and finding faults with others, yet secretly love to find the wrongdoing for which we seek in the world, its leaders, and a country's infrastructure—how, indeed, nothing works right. Above all, we obsess with finding fault with our own bodies. That is why we made our dream to be such that the body would not only be imperfect, but would sicken, age, deteriorate, and eventually stop functioning altogether.

We all know how we love to complain to each other—family, friends, co-workers, even strangers—about how our bodies fail us: We don't sleep or eat

well, digest or eliminate well, relate to others well—
we don't do anything well. We are obsessed with the
body and its obvious failings—as individuals and as
societies. Read any newspaper or listen to any news
broadcast—there are always complaints about someone or something. We say that the world does not
work right, even though it should—the comparison
disguising the attack that underlies everything we do
here. The judgment, once again, is that we hold others
responsible for our defective nature and the defects in
the world.

The world as a whole is a gigantic subterfuge to
keep from our awareness the fact that *we*—our
decision-making minds—did this. Near the end of
Chapter 27 we are told: "The secret of salvation is
but this: that you are doing this unto yourself"
(T-27.VIII.10:1). It is not the world that is limited, but
our minds, limited by the decision that denied our
power over the limitation. That was Epictetus' point:
You cannot change the world, but you can certainly
change how you react to it. For this wise philosopher,
the virtuous ones were those who looked at things in
a different way, and did not let the world affect how
they felt inside. Jesus says the same thing to us in
A Course in Miracles. We are the rulers of the universe
(e.g., W-pII.253): We cannot change the physical universe, but we can change how we look at it. "Therefore," Jesus tells us, "seek not to change the world, but

choose to change your mind about the world" (T-21.in.1:7). Since the world is nothing more than a projection of our own thinking, and we *can* do something about our thinking by choosing differently, we rule our universe. No one else has that power, unless we give it away. Yet if I give the power to you or anyone else, *I* am the one who gave it, which means I still have it. I may not have power over your body, but I have power over how I react to your body. Yours may be able to do all kinds of things to mine, but you can do nothing to my mind. The only one who has that power is me—not God, the Holy Spirit, Jesus, or the ego—which leaves only the decision-making part of the mind in control. It is the power of which Jesus continually reminds us. Again, when we become disturbed because of the shadows of limitations in our body and the world, we are giving the power to someone or something outside us.

It is essential to understand that we are the ones who chose limitation, and therefore we are the only ones who can undo it. Until that choice is made, this world *will* imprison us. Indeed, to the wrong mind the world *is* a prison, with the body being a mini-prison because it is a limitation, the same as the bars on a jail cell. Yet the body is a limitation only as long as we think we are one. If we were an actual prisoner in a cell, we would of course be limited by the cell's bars that prevent our getting out—a fact within the world.

Inmates in a death camp are kept prisoners by the guards and can do nothing about their external situation. Their minds, however, cannot be imprisoned by the guards or the bars, nor by the limited and deteriorating body. The mind's love cannot be limited by a diseased organ or a diseased social or political situation, but the body can. Our genes make the body what it is: healthy or not healthy; masculine or feminine; tall or short; black or white; brown or blue eyed. However, this makes no difference to the mind unless it identifies with the body, wherein it can make a tremendous difference. Thus people become obsessed with changing their bodies—making them stronger, younger, older, healthier, prettier, thinner, or heavier. All these attempts make perfect sense once we have identified with the physical, as would our trying to change the world. Yet once we shift identification to the mind, our orientation becomes entirely different, for the only thing we would seek to change would be thought systems. The hallmark of this change is our attitude of non-judgment—acceptance of the external by changing the internal. In this way, an adverse world made sour by bitterness becomes sweet by the kind and gentle love of our new teacher.

2. "Sweet Are the Uses of Adversity"

Our teacher Jesus helps us by shifting our perception of the body's limitations and the world in which the body lives—from prison to classroom. Some lovely verses in Shakespeare's early comedy, *As You Like It*, are the inspiration for this chapter. The context of these verses, one phrase of which gives this chapter its title, is the reaction of the duke to his banishment to the forest, having had his realm usurped by his unscrupulous younger brother. Not succumbing to discouragement or despair, the duke finds that exile is not so bad after all—for one thing, he does not have to deal with the burdens of being in court. The duke says:

> *Sweet are the uses of adversity;*
>
> *..*
>
> *And this our life, exempt from public haunt,*
> *Finds tongues in trees, books in the running brooks,*
> *Sermons in stones and good in everything:*
> *I would not change it.*

One of his lords responds:

> *Happy is your Grace,*
> *That can translate the stubbornness of fortune*
> *Into so quiet and so sweet a style.*

(II,i)

These kind and healing sentiments find a parallel in a passage near the end of the text where Jesus tells us:

> Trials are but lessons that you failed to learn presented once again, so where you made a faulty choice before you now can make a better one, and thus escape all pain that what you chose before has brought to you (T-31.VIII.3:1).

What is noteworthy about this little speech is that Shakespeare does not say "How sweet is adversity," but "How sweet are the *uses* of adversity." The same with *A Course in Miracles*—nowhere does Jesus say the world is a good thing, or sweet. In fact, he pointedly says the opposite as he paints for us a rather bleak picture of our home, never seeking to sugar-coat or paint a pretty face on it. He simply exposes to us what the world is like, being an attack on God (W-pII. 3.2:1). However, although it is a place of hell, suffering, and death—because it comes from a thought of hell, suffering, and death—the world can still serve a sweet use, a different purpose: translated from the prison that the ego uses to enslave us, into a classroom in which Jesus teaches us his happy lessons of forgiveness. Those lessons, then, would be "sweet," and so the duke's lord comments that his master is happy because he "can translate the stubbornness of fortune into so quiet and so sweet a style."

The point here is that when we live according to our right minds, with Jesus or the Holy Spirit as our Teacher, we live by the principle of acceptance— accepting the world as it is and our lives of limitation without trying to change them. This is an important step that cannot be skipped without negative conse- quences for our spiritual progress. In the text, Jesus states that "the ego analyzes; the Holy Spirit accepts" (T-11.V.13:1). The ego made a brain that seemingly governs the body because the brain is the instrument of analysis. It is what we believe thinks, reasons, and understands, taking the sensory data that the ego pro- grammed our sensory organs to bring back, and synthesizes them to produce a conclusion that we think makes sense and, most insanely, that we act upon. In essence, we take illusory information to which we give an illusory explanation, and then be- lieve this to be reality, which then becomes the basis of our response and reaction.

The Holy Spirit, on the other hand, does not ana- lyze. He simply accepts what is true. This translates in our personal experience to accepting what alone is true in the world of illusion: nothing here has the power to bring us pleasure or pain, happiness or grief. In the process of reaching that level, however, we need be sure that we not avoid recognizing that the world is indeed a horrid place, where we live out the horrid intention in our minds of limiting love to our specifications of specialness. The world's only value —a huge value, to be sure—is that it displays for us what is in our minds. What needs correction and healing is the mind's mistaken decision to identify with the ego instead of the Holy Spirit, and our guilt and fear stem from that mistaken choice. Looking at the *mindless* world through Jesus' eyes shows us this mistake so we can *mindfully* choose again.

This corrected vision reflects the important Course principle *projection makes perception*. Without question, projection is the most important concept to understand in order to apply the teachings of *A Course in Miracles*. The text in general, and the early workbook lessons specifically, are about projection—the ego's belief that ideas leave their source. The Holy Spirit's correction that *ideas leave not their source* undoes this ego dynamic by showing that what we perceive outside comes from what is inside. This "inside" is not an amorphous psyche or brain, but the mind. Recall that what gives me access to my mind is paying attention to what goes on in my bodily life: what I feel about a news program, situation, or person—my projected imperfections and limitations. If I am not at peace, I have chosen the ego. *A Course in Miracles* helps me realize not only *that* I have done that, but *why* I have done so: I do not want to be at peace, because without conflict I will cease to be the unfairly treated self I see as my identity.

The world then becomes a classroom with significant meaning for us, but not because of its inherent value—it has none. It is important to accept the world of limitations—collective and personal—because that is our only entrée to accepting what we have chosen in our minds. We accept "the stubbornness of [our] fortune," as Shakespeare's duke did, but now with a purpose that is quiet and sweet, because forgiveness is quiet and sweet.

The adversity we associate with our limitations is chosen as a defense against the peace-filled happiness of being a child of God. Sweet, indeed, are the uses of adversity when we look at the limitations we chose and now choose again, not by changing the body or the external situation, but by changing the purpose of the body and the situation. Rather than being a defense, they become the means of our returning to the mind, that we may choose again. In Shakespeare's play, the duke, as would any good stoic, accepted his fate; he did not launch a counter-invasion against his younger brother. In the play, everything ends up fine; yet regardless of a situation's outcome, we can be at peace. If we were in the duke's place, perhaps we would be guided to conquer the land that had been seized from us. But if we followed that course of action, we would do so with no investment in the outcome, and without hatred or a desire for vengeance.

I mentioned above the parallel to the duke's speech at the end of the text. Here is the next line in that passage:

> In every difficulty, all distress, and each perplexity
> Christ calls to you and gently says, "My brother,
> choose again" (T-31.VIII.3:2).

Jesus is not denying that we would experience difficulty, distress, or perplexity. That is why, to say it again, it is psychologically disastrous, not to mention deleterious to our spiritual growth to deny negative experiences. Rather than feel guilty, angry, or depressed about a problem—physical or psychological—we need to accept it as a classroom, telling ourselves this is the form in which we will learn what we need to learn: whatever the distress, it is our choosing. This is not because we are neurotic, psychotic, or bad, but because we want to prove we are who we are not; that the separated, sinful, and guilty self is real, and our glorious Self an illusion. Whatever its form, we are simply using the distress to prove the reality of the separation. Anything that we feel robs us of peace—our imperfections or those of others, circumstances beyond our control—can now serve a different purpose we should welcome. Rather than fight against the symptom, problem, or situation —we need embrace it, not because it has value in and of itself, but because of the purpose it will now serve.

That very defect, imperfection, or adverse situation is the classroom Jesus can use to teach this is all in the mind. Not only that, it is in the mind because we want it to be there. If we agonize about something, repress it, drown it out, argue with it, or feel guilty over it, we deprive Jesus of the classroom he needs in order to teach us. After all, a teacher cannot teach without a classroom or curriculum.

Thus our limitations, symptoms, and problems are the curricula for Jesus' classroom, and our teacher wants us to welcome them in a spirit of acceptance rather than agonizing over them. To repeat this central lesson, if we despair over our limitations, we deny Jesus his only means of helping us. We would do that only because we do not want his help and do not want to learn from him. Why else would we deny him the classroom? Everything is purposive, even if it docs not appear to be so. Becoming upset is thus a way of pushing Jesus away—*un*inviting him, as it were.

We therefore need to welcome him into the classrooms of our lives so he can help us realize where the upset is truly coming from. If we make a big deal about what we see as a neurotic symptom or limitation, we fragment our lives. Being in the world is *the* neurotic symptom, while being in a body is *the* inherent limitation of our self. Why should we select certain limitations to agonize over when our entire existence is a limitation? For example, our eyesight is a limitation because our eyes were made not to see (e.g., T-22.III.6:1; T-28.V.4:8). One could not ask for a better example of a limitation. Real seeing—Christ's vision—occurs in the mind when we join with the Holy Spirit. Yet we made eyes that are severely limited *because* they cannot see. Indeed, Jesus refers to our sightless eyes (e.g., T-24.V.7:3; T-25.V.2:11; W-pI.121.4:2). Our ears, too, are a limitation, for the only meaningful "hearing" is listening to the Holy Spirit's Voice as the correction for having listened to the voice of the ego. Instead of hearing truly, we make ears and then believe we hear sounds, which are not really there.

Moreover, we make a fuss over someone born with a limited brain that thinks with an IQ of 70 instead of 120—as if that were really different from being born with eyes. One might object that everyone has eyes, but some eyes see better than others, and some ears hear better than others. Animals see, hear, and smell differently from us; yet they, too, are seeing things, hearing sounds, and smelling odors that are not there. Remember, the body itself is a limitation. An arm weakened by disease or a brain limited by a chromosomal defect are no different from being born with a healthy body. Recall Jesus' statement in the text that the body is a limit on love, made to limit the unlimited (T-18.VIII.1:2-3). His lesson to us is that regardless of the limitation, we can learn to see and think, but not with our eyes and brain.

It is helpful to recognize that we have an investment in focusing on specific symptoms, because as long as we do—agonizingly and despairingly—we but do what the ego wants: protecting ourselves from Jesus' teaching. We compound this arrogance by then asking him to help us, when we are really pushing him away. The help we beseech him for at that point is magic, not a miracle, for the latter changes the mind, while the former changes the body's symptoms— Jesus is a teacher of miracles, not a magician. Watch, therefore, how you focus on specific problems, limitations, and symptoms, whether in yourself or others. Anything that fragments is of the ego, for its thought system is rooted in fragmentation, as Jesus describes in "The Substitute Reality" (T-18.I).

In speaking of difficulty, distress, and perplexity, Jesus indicates to us that he knows our lives are not particularly easy. He helps us to know, in the midst of our dis-ease, that we can look at everything differently. To return to the duke's speech, "Sweet are the uses of adversity," Jesus would not change the adversity, but rather help us change the *use* we make of it. When Jesus says, "My brother, choose again," he is not telling us to choose a different form; he is advising us to choose a different way of *looking* at the form. Remember, if you focus on changing the external you have made it real, which means you have again walked into the ego's trap. The ego wants to make the world's and the body's problems real, because that keeps us mindless, protecting the ego from the mind's power to choose. In this regard it is important not to lose sight of the fact that the ego is us—the part of the mind that likes being separated, special, and unique. This part fears the mind's decision maker—the one thing in the universe with the power to undo the ego. Thus, choosing again means the mind choosing a different teacher, who reassuringly tells us:

> The images you make cannot prevail against what God Himself would have you be (T-31. VIII.4:1).

If God or Jesus were to be involved with helping you with problems, that would make them real, which means you would not be as God created you. Consider that if God created you as Christ, Who has no problems, to insist that Jesus help you with your problems is to demand he share your shabby self-image, seeing you the way *you* see you—a vulnerable self beset with problems—and not as the Self that God created. Be grateful, then, that he does nothing in the world, because if he did, he would not be the sublime symbol of God's Love, for he would have seen you as a problem-laden ego. Yet, again, that is how you insist Jesus see you every time you ask for specific help, and why he told Helen not to ask him to help her take away her fear (T-2.VI.4:1-3). That would have been the worst thing she could have done, for it would have gone against the Course's purpose of returning to us the power of the mind to choose. Jesus thus says to us all: "You choose to see yourselves as having problems, and I can help you look at these, but cannot help you with what you perceive to be true. The fact is that you do not have problems, except in thinking that you do." That is how Jesus teaches us that nothing has the power to separate us from the Love of God in our minds, for despite our limitations and imperfections —projected onto the body—we remain the one Son that God created one with Him. Forgiving limitations —in ourselves or in others—clears away the interference to remembering our oneness with each other, with ourselves, and with our Creator.

3. "One Brother Is All Brothers" – No Exceptions

One of the main objectives of this discussion is that we come to recognize how easily and quickly we judge, and how we use the teachings of *A Course in Miracles* to reinforce these judgments. A helpful rule of thumb to follow is that if what you say about someone is not true of absolutely everyone, it must be from your ego, and is an attack—*no exceptions*. We all share the same wrong-minded thought system—*no exceptions*. We all share the same right-minded thought system—*no exceptions*. We all share the same power to choose between them—*no exceptions*. This is true for everyone—*no exceptions*. When you speak of specific limitations you have fallen into judgment, which means you are hearing the ego's voice. You have made the judgment to listen to the ego, which you pass on as if it had nothing to do with you. Whether you speak of perceptual or meta-physical facts, you are separating and limiting the Sonship. Making no exceptions to your evaluations is a helpful guide that enables you not to take anything you or anyone else thinks seriously.

It does not matter whether you attack, praise, or give spiritual meaning to limitations—your own or anyone else's. Specialness is specialness. Whenever you make an evaluation of a limitation that does not

45

embrace the whole Sonship, it is of the ego and will only breed further ego thoughts. The Stoic attitude that Epictetus fostered was equanimity and peace regardless of what befell him, the same vision Jesus holds out to us: to be at peace regardless of what goes on around us. Something works out or does not; an anticipated telephone call, letter, or check comes, or it does not; a person you love says yes or no—when in your right mind, none of this has any effect on your peace.

Our situation is like going to class in the morning and asking the teacher: "Jesus, what am I to learn today?" He answers that we always learn the same thing—all we ever need know—and the forms in which learning occurs are irrelevant. What did I learn yesterday? What will I learn today and tomorrow? *Forgiveness*. One lesson may occur in relationship with my body, another with yours or that of a public figure. It is irrelevant what the day presents to us—and it presents only the mind's unconscious script, for we write the curriculum—because the lesson's content is the same. Though coming from different metaphysical premises, Epictetus and Jesus encourage the same equanimity.

Whether you encounter someone expressing love or calling for it—regardless of the form—your response remains love. Even if the calling for love takes an attacking or abusive form, the right-minded content of your response is the same. The lesson is that the form makes no difference, and this is the meaning of Jesus' New Year's prayer at the end of Chapter 15: "Make this year different by making it all the same" (T-15.XI.10:11). We make this year different from all the others by having everything—this year and every year—be the same, which means the mind's responses to all situations are one, for their right-minded purpose is one.

Everything that goes on in your life carries the same lesson: to see a shadow as a shadow, not reality. If you see it as a shadow you will not react to it, in the sense of giving it power to take away your peace. If you see someone else reacting to the shadow, meaning that person is confusing appearance and reality, shadow and truth, your response will simply be—*in content, not necessarily in form*—to point out that a shadow has no effect on your love and peace. Thus, regardless of what that person's belief in shadows is doing to your body or the bodies of those with whom you identify, your response is still loving and peaceful. That response of love and peace—*thoughts in your mind*—will take whatever shape is most helpful. The shape is irrelevant, as only the content is important. That makes your life simple and consistent, because it does not matter what is done around you. You are still at peace.

In this state of mind, the only sane response to a shadow of limitation is to look beyond it to the light. Every shadow, to paraphrase *A Course in Miracles*, is a call for the light that has been denied; every attack is an expression of fear, which itself is a call for love. When that is your perception—the Holy Spirit's true perception or Christ's vision—nothing here will affect you. Either you will see people expressing the light, or being caught in the shadows that call for the light. Regardless, you let the light in your mind shine forth, in whatever form is most helpful.

It is important to keep in mind that the above rule of thumb applies only to *content*, not *form*. You certainly can make statements about people's forms that are not true of everyone—not everyone is male or female, for example. People differ in eye, skin, and hair color, not to mention personalities. Our behavior clearly differs as well: some are reading this book sitting at a desk, in an easy chair, laying in bed, or walking. All these are perceptual facts within the perceptual universe, but have nothing to do with anything real. It is the content alone that is meaningful, for everyone reading this book—indeed, everyone in the world—has a wrong mind, right mind, and decision maker that chooses between the two. That is the only true statement one can make within the world of illusion.

You need to notice how you respond to the form as though it were the content, as though it were reality. This is not to say you should not have a point of view— political, ethical, religious, etc. It simply means that you do not let that point of view assume the power to accentuate differences and separation. Having a point of view is simply an aspect of the shadowy world of judgments and distinctions that we inhabit. Try not to forget that the world of separation began when we labelled the tiny, mad idea a sin, and no longer thought of it as a shadow, making it into an evil thing performed by an evil-doer that had to be punished. Once we, as one Son, took the impossible thought seriously, we were off and running, and we have continued to run ever since—to hell and still deeper into its pits of despair and death.

Because of our ego's response, Jesus asks us to shift from seeing the world as a prison to a classroom, in which we look at the manifestations of the tiny, mad idea—everything in the world—and regard them as but shadows of an illusion. However, these are but the absence of light, and we need to become aware of the pain of living in a world that is the absence of light, truth, and love. This pain will eventually motivate us to declare: "I do not want to live in darkness, but in the light. I do not want to remain a prisoner in Plato's cave and look only to the shadowy images on the wall, but instead to look to the light of truth." We cannot know there is a light, however, until we are first instructed by our new teacher that what we are perceiving as real is only a shadow. When we judge the limitation—the tiny, mad idea—saying it is a reality that is good or bad, we have judged God and rejected His perfect Oneness. Jesus continually reminds us that special love and special hate are the same—whether we love or hate something, it is still a something. The minute we feel a charge in us about anything or anyone, that is the red flag that should make us stop and return to the mind, saying to Jesus: "Please help me. I have again gotten caught in the shadow, believing it to be reality."

A Course in Miracles helps us understand why we get caught in the shadow and believe it to be real: We do not want to hear that the self we spent so many years cultivating and defending is an illusion. We want to be told it is a real substance, and beyond that, it is a substance that has been caused by something else—the cause of our unhappiness and distress. With every fiber of our ego's being, we resist learning we are shadows and that all the seeming limitations in the world are shadows as well. Its defects, faults, sins, mistakes, and the things people do that we like or dislike are simply shadows that have the same cause: the absence of light. As Jesus' students, we learn that the response to shadow is light, the response to attack is love, the response to separation is Atonement—and he is our response to the ego.

Once you understand the principle, you spend the rest of your life putting it into practice. Day in and day out you become aware of how you get caught in the ego's shadowy traps, how your feelings get aroused, seemingly beyond your control, by what ends up being simply shadows of illusions. When you get upset about a limitation, however, it is no longer seen as a shadow, for you become chained in Plato's cave of ignorance once again, and all you see are the figures on the wall. Because you see nothing else, you believe these shadows are reality, and then you judge them— some tall, others short; some you like, others you do not. As I said above, however, anything you say about someone that cannot be generalized to the Sonship as a whole is an illusion, and therefore an attack. Yet this does not involve *form*. Do not deny what your physical eyes see, but let Jesus teach you not to take what your physical eyes see seriously. As I mentioned earlier, the Course says several times—explicitly and implicitly—that our eyes do not see. Recalling that helps us not take seriously anything our eyes see, our ears hear, or our brains interpret.

Granted, when you watch a news broadcast, it is rather difficult not to have a reaction to what goes on, whether it is happening in Washington, the Middle

East, or Africa. However, I once again do not speak of a point of view, but of an emotional reaction that disrupts your peace. This should help you realize you do not want to walk out of Plato's cave but wish to remain there, with someone else as the imprisoning agent. You do not yet want to see that *you* are the imprisoning agent, holding the key that would unlock the binding chains of guilt. Your day, therefore, should be a classroom in which Jesus teaches you to redefine limitations—your personal limitations as well as those you see around you. What you see are merely shadows. Their forms are legion, but they all contain the same illusory content.

Lesson 161 speaks to this principle of generalization, acknowledging the difficulty in both comprehending that we are one and in applying this vision to our daily lives. With great clarity Jesus tells us the truth—we are all one—and at the same time helps us apply it with gentleness and patience. This combination of unambiguous statements of truth, and yet kind and gentle application of that truth is one of the aspects of *A Course in Miracles* that makes it unique among world spiritualities. Here is the passage:

> One brother is all brothers. Every mind contains all minds, for every mind is one. Such is the truth. Yet do these thoughts make clear the meaning of creation? Do these words bring perfect clarity

with them to you? What can they seem to be but empty sounds; pretty, perhaps, correct in sentiment, yet fundamentally not understood nor understandable. The mind that taught itself to think specifically can no longer grasp abstraction in the sense that it is all-encompassing. We need to see a little, that we learn a lot (W-pI.161.4).

Jesus begins with one of the central metaphysical ideas in his course—one mind is all minds —and then proceeds to tell us we do not have a clue as to what he is talking about: lovely words and sentiments, but meaningless to us because of the barrage of needs and demands that impinge on us—bodies having to deal with other bodies. Above all, we are creatures of specifics, which Jesus spoke of in the two preceding paragraphs of this lesson. Non-specificity is the natural condition of the mind (2:1), he said; but that is essentially irrelevant to our experience as specific bodies with specific personalities, members of specific races, religions, cultures, and nationalities, practicing specific spiritualities and religions. Moreover, we actually believe there is a Jesus whose mind is separate from ours and speaks to us. How, then, could we possibly know the nature of oneness? Our closest approximation comes in realizing that we share one purpose, for we share the same insanity and the need to be healed of it. *That* we can be taught to understand.

Jesus concludes this paragraph with the words "We need to see a little, that we learn a lot," which exemplifies the gentleness of his approach. He starts us off with where we believe we are—in our specific (read: special) relationships. My specific body is in a specific relationship with yours, and Jesus teaches me that what goes on between us has nothing to do with *us*, the relationship being a projection of the mind's decision: my special relationship with you mirrors my special relationship with my ego. I first realize this is true with you, and then realize it is also true with others—indeed, it is true with everyone. As I practice with the "little" specifics and learn to generalize, I come to learn "a lot."

This specifically means that I recognize that you and I share the same purpose. Each of us desperately calls out to be proven wrong about our insane thinking. Somewhere inside me is a thought of sanity, but I cannot reach it if you do not first attack me and make me feel guilty. This eventually leads to my choosing against my guilt, which your projection revealed for me. Thus you have become an instrument pointing me in the direction of that sanity, as I do for you. We all walk around with the same plea: "Please show me there is hope, by showing me I am wrong."

Your attack shows me this, and I demonstrate the hope by not attacking back, defensively seeing my interests as separate from yours. To the extent to which

I can be defenseless, I represent the thought of sanity that is in everyone's mind. That is Jesus' point, saying to us in effect: "The sanity in my mind is in yours as well"—the meaning of the statement that we were with him when he arose (C-6.5:5). When he awoke from the dream of death—having nothing to do with physical resurrection—we were with him because one mind is every mind; each mind contains all minds. This means that if Jesus' mind is healed, ours is, too. The problem is that we have not accepted the healing that is there. Yet to the extent to which we allow Jesus to look at our ego with us, to be present in our minds, to that extent we will begin to think as he does, growing to become like him in kindness and love. And so his very presence of light—simply by being there, not doing or saying anything—is what continually calls us to walk out of the darkness with him, bringing our brothers with us through our forgiveness.

Q: If I react to a limitation but catch it, is it productive to just realize that I have been mistaken as to who I am? Would that be sufficient to give it to the decision maker as opposed to the body?

A: The answer is "yes"; but an important part of that "yes" is realizing *why* you made the limitation real. You must accept that there is a purpose behind your madness, to recall the famous line from *Hamlet*. The method in your madness in choosing the limitation is that it keeps you here, while blaming someone else for it. You must understand—otherwise this process will never work—that choosing this has cost you happiness: the pain of keeping you away from the love that part of you really wants, for that is what you are. Your mistaken choice has also kept you away from Jesus, for you fear that, being with his love, *you* will disappear. The ego's bottom line is preserving the self by making someone else responsible for the loss of Self. This is why we have bodies, and why we make them reproduce the way they do—some other bodies made us; our birth was not our doing.

The fear is that if I get in touch with the fact that *I* made me, my mind will be overwhelmed with guilt, and rather than look within and choose differently, I make the guilt real, project it, and then see everyone else as responsible for my misery. It is only when I return to the mind that I can recognize that the guilt was a decision I made, testifying to my sin that says I have separated and now exist. Guilt, then, becomes one of the ego's most powerful ways of defending against learning that I do *not* exist—I am not separated and did not sin. Nothing happened, for the Oneness of God and His Son remain undivided: one Son is all Sons—*no exceptions.*

The Limitations of Sickness and Aging

Q: One form of limitation is physical pain. In my case, I cannot get around well because of my condition, which is an even further limitation. I am aware that this is all a shadow or a limitation, and that just seems to induce guilt, which seems to accelerate the physical pain.[*]

A: One of the areas with which students of *A Course in Miracles* have the greatest trouble is sickness. On the one hand, it is helpful to know that the mind makes the body sick. On a practical level, which is where we should always begin, think of our friend Epictetus and simply accept that your body is sick. As we get older we almost inevitably become more infirm and clearly cannot do what we did thirty, forty, or fifty years ago. When you are sick, therefore, do whatever you can to minimize the pain; but you can do so either in peace and equanimity, or with anger, resentment, and guilt. The point is not to focus on having the perfect body, nor crucifying yourself because you are getting older. In so many words, the answer is that you should not become upset. As you deal with your body as best you can, at the same time

[*] This topic is also discussed in *Releasing Judgment*, Volume One of *The Healing Power of Kindness*.

watch your reactions, and see if you react calmly, saying: "My body is in pain today, and there are various things I should do about it." And then proceed, but in peace instead of with agitation, anxiety, or anger.

The last thing you want is to slam yourself with a judgment seemingly based upon *A Course in Miracles*: "Sickness is a defense against the truth, and I am a terrible person because I am defending against it." All you then do is set up a hierarchy of illusions. Yes, your sickness is a defense against the truth, but so is breathing, or seeing through your eyes. There *is* no hierarchy of illusions, the ego's first law of chaos notwithstanding. The first principle of miracles—"There is no order of difficulty among them" (T-1.I.1:1)—teaches that every illusion is the same. These first principles of the ego and the Holy Spirit are the foundations for their respective thought systems. The other four laws of chaos are derived from the first, and if you were to understand the first miracle principle, you would not have to read the other forty-nine, nor the rest of the text. You would get an exemption from the workbook, too, because the first principle contains the entirety of the Holy Spirit's thought system—everything is an illusion: a shadow is a shadow is a shadow.

If you are tempted to judge yourself because you are having trouble getting out of bed in the morning, do not make an exception; remind yourself: "I should then also feel guilty because I am breathing." That is true of everyone. Maybe not everyone is having the same trouble getting out of bed—but that is only form. Everyone here thinks he or she is a body, which means everyone here is trying to limit love. Your physical condition is just another expression of that secret wish. If you recognize your symptoms as but a form of the tiny, mad idea, you would realize that your choice is not whether or not to be in pain. The issue is whether to look at the pain through the eyes of the ego, which leads you to maximize its importance, or through the eyes of the Holy Spirit, which leads you to see it as the day's classroom, and perhaps one for the rest of your life. Your only focus should be on which teacher you invite into your mind: the one that will make the shadow real—guilt and judgment always do so—or the teacher who will help you realize this is a shadow that has no effect on the peace of God within you. By forgiving the mistake of choosing the limitations of the ego, we learn to forgive everyone and everything—*without exception.*

Remember that the second half of the workbook's Introduction discusses generalizing what you learned in any one lesson about your particular shadow of limitation to every relationship and circumstance in which you find yourself. It not only is true that it is a lie to say something about a person that is not true of everyone, but it is also part of the ego's delusional thought system to say something about a circumstance that you do not generalize to all circumstances. A major sickness is no different from a minor one; a disagreement with your spouse is no different from being on the verge of World War III—the content remains the same. It makes no difference what it looks like. One times zero is no different in the end from a thousand times zero. How many times are you going to multiply nothing and think you will get an answer that is something? And so, if you do not look at any one situation the way you would look at every situation, you know you have again chosen the ego because you are seeing distinctions. Having seen differentiation, you have made separation real, meaning you have made the shadows of limitation real and cannot then be free of them.

Q: As we get older, our bodies seem to fail us, and I understand that it is really my mind's doing. But how come my decision maker chooses the form of pain increasing as I grow older?

A: This establishes that we are victims of the body's old age—another way of making the body real. Don't look at your aging body any differently than you would look at any other issue in your life. It is but another form of worshipping the body, an example of how the ego has made up a world of limitations as a way of saying you are a prisoner of these shadows, which makes them real to us. Aging is only a fact in the dream. You can be at peace even when your body does not function the way it functioned several years ago. You simply say to yourself: "My body breaking down is but a fact within the dream; but what does that have to do with my inner peace?" That is the lesson. In principle, of course, one could live to an old age without any deterioration or infirmity, but the fact that you do not does not make you good or bad. Try to resist the temptation to judge according to form. Some people will age more gracefully than others, as they are a different shadow than others. The trap is in judging the *content* by the *form*, for you do not know where that particular shadow fits into the person's greater Atonement path. You cannot know their lessons on the level of *form*, but you can, and do know everyone's lesson in *content*, for it is the same as yours.

Q: It seems as if we are living in a culture that turns its back on old people—not wanting to deal with them nor look on death. When you were talking about acceptance I was thinking how much easier it would be if we just said: "Well, that's what happens. People get old; they have strokes; they get walkers; they take pills; they die. What's the big deal?" But there's such a struggle in me; I don't want to look at it.

A: What you describe is people making the body real, and thus its fate is so terrible that they agonize over it or simply deny it. Yet this is all based on the idea that life in the body is truly life, and what happens to it is important. Since we are told by the ego that we are the body and we need to maintain our existence, preserving the body takes on value. As *A Course in Miracles* emphasizes, death is one of the core thoughts in the ego system (M-27.1:1), because if death is real, life obviously has to be as well. If so, then God's life is not. The death of the body thus proves its reality, not to mention the thought system that gave it birth. Once you make the body real you cannot win, because either you worry about the body or deny it. One way or another, the body is center stage—as described in "The 'Hero' of the Dream" (T-27.VIII), where the body is the hero of every dream the world has had.

Given this insanity, it is saner and more helpful to accept what happens: bodies do age and things do go wrong here. You attend to the body, for it is silly to be in pain when it is not necessary. Yet your focus should not be on preserving the body, as is seen today in the inordinate emphasis placed on living longer. This quest to prolong life is absurd when you step back with Jesus and recognize that the body is only a classroom, with no meaning outside the mind's purpose. Therefore, watch in kindness and gentleness how you get caught in the ego system time and time again. When you are in your right mind, the body ceases to be a pre-occupation. It is there, to be sure, and you take care of it until you are ready to let it go, when it dies. Yet this is not the end of the mind or your Atonement path—only the end of this particular segment of the dream. Living another ten, twenty, or thirty years is nothing, for you can learn the lesson in one day or one minute. Again, you merely watch your bodily identification, which is really an ego identification. When concerns arise around your body or those of loved ones, recognize these concerns are not what you think. Do with them exactly what you would with anything else, but look with Jesus at what your ego is doing. Preoccupation with the body is number one on the ego's list, because that is its primary defense—the home of the special relationship, wherein the mind's dynamics are acted out, though we are unaware of its existence.

And so, do whatever feels right with your body, but watch your obsession with it, realizing this is not about what you think—your age or illness—but about anything that would distract you from remembering you are a decision-making mind. Continue to obsess, and don't fight against it or ignore it, but do step back and recognize what it truly is and where it comes from. Only then can your body serve the kind purpose of healing Jesus has given it, the means whereby he leads us home through forgiveness—our special function.

4. "The Special Function": The Detour That Leads Us Home

Our previous discussions highlight the gospel injunction that we should be *in* the world but not *of* it, which goes to the heart of the message of *A Course in Miracles*. We are not asked to deny what goes on in the world, nor what we think, feel, see, or hear, but only to look differently at these sensory perceptions. After all, the *miracle* that lends its name to this course is a shift in perception. When Jesus talks about looking through Christ's vision, he refers to a thought system we choose in our minds. In fact, everything is in our minds, since *ideas leave not their source*. The ego, therefore, views the world in terms of its relevance for reinforcing judgment and affirming limitations in ourselves and others—with the sole purpose of proving we are different from each other, just as we became different from God in the separation. This has nothing to do with what our eyes see, but rather with how we interpret what they see. In the Course, *perception* means interpretation, and Jesus teaches us that the problem was not the tiny, mad idea, but the way we perceived it, choosing the ego's way of looking over the Holy Spirit's. The choice we had then is the choice we have now, because there is no "then" and "now" in the mind. Linear time exists only in the projected image of a world of sin, guilt, and fear—past, present, and future. In the mind they are one:

> Each day, and every minute in each day, and every instant that each minute holds, you but relive the single instant when the time of terror took the place of love.... Such is each life; a seeming interval from birth to death and on to life again, a repetition of an instant gone by long ago that cannot be relived. And all of time is but the mad belief that what is over is still here and now (T-26.V.13:1,3-4).

At the beginning, we—God's one Son—had a choice between two mutually exclusive ways of perceiving the tiny, mad idea: through the eyes of judgment (sin) or Atonement (forgiveness); the latter sees nothing to forgive because nothing happened—the tiny, mad idea was an impossibility. It is this principle we are asked to carry into the daily experiences that constitute our dream. The miracle shifts us from the ego's way of looking, which perceives separate interests: you and I are at war, resulting in a winner and loser. This blocks the Holy Spirit's correction: the right-minded view that we share the same interests. To restate the rule of thumb I have discussed above, try never to make a judgment about someone—in *content*, not *form*—that does not apply to all. The perception of the Holy Spirit, or Christ's vision, sees everyone as the same, regardless of differences in appearance.

Earlier I cited the Course statement that what the ego made to harm, the Holy Spirit uses to heal. The very limitations we made to prove God wrong and us right—indeed, that we exist and the true God is non-existent—become the very thing Jesus uses to lead us home. When we chose the ego over the Holy Spirit, we established our own kingdom and embarked on a long and horrendous journey that the Course refers to as the ladder separation led us down (T-28.III.1), or the mad course into insanity (T-18.I.7:6). This journey, then, becomes the means, when we change teachers, to awaken us from the dream. Taking this perspective will help us avoid judging ourselves or others for the foolish things we do. Recall that we share the same insanity and viciousness, and so the very things we did to attack God, deny His reality, and establish our own in its place, become holy—not for themselves, but because inviting a different Teacher into the classroom of our lives allows them to serve a holy purpose. In the Holy Spirit's perception, everything here, no matter where it falls on society's continuum of good and evil, is seen as a detour—a roundabout way of returning to Heaven. Indeed, every pathway, relationship, or script we have written will eventually lead us home, if we choose the right Guide. After all, detours that confront us when we are driving do lead us to our destination, if we follow the signs that lead us through the problem. Likewise, our special relationships will lead us to our spiritual destination, if we follow the signposts of forgiveness that Jesus illuminates to help us navigate our way through the problem of limitations.

These detours, in effect, constitute the contours of our lives. The only difference is that before, we went away from Heaven, and now we reverse our course— literally, we choose a different *course*—and ascend the ladder separation led us down. To be sure, it is a detour because it is not the direct route; how could it be with our fear of return so great? That is why Jesus comforts us: "Fear not that you will be abruptly lifted up and hurled into reality" (T-16.VI.8:1). Later in the text, he says we do not go straight from nightmares to reality but move through the various steps called happy or gentle dreams (T-20.VIII.10; T-27.VII.13). These are the detours of our special relationships, but blessed with the Holy Spirit's purpose of forgiveness. In the end, since time and space are an illusion, it makes no difference how long it took to get home, or how devious the route. When we arrive, the carpet of time—our detours—rolls up behind us and disappears (T-13.I.3:5): "The outcome is as certain as God" (T-2.III.3:10).

Since the special liabilities and limitations we built into the ego self become the contours that shape the

68

direction of our return home, judging them—starving them through various forms of asceticism or abuse, or making fun of ourselves or others—but places road-blocks that sabotage our way. It would be as if we deliberately made potholes in the road to get a flat tire—hindering the vehicle that will take us to our destination. And so we are not asked in this course to give up our special relationships, deficiencies, or defects—*only to give them a different purpose*. The very things that brought us so much pain become the means to lead us beyond it.

What is required is to let go of the ego as our teacher. Two separate lines in the Course read like this when put together: "Resign now as your own teacher, for you have been badly taught" (T-12.V.8:3; T-28.I.7:1). We resign by firing the ego and bringing in the Holy Spirit. He does not change our lives, however, as is explained in "Are Changes Required in the Life Situation of God's Teachers?" (M-9), for only the inner change—from the ego to the Holy Spirit—is important. Jesus tells us in the text that the Holy Spirit does not take away the special relationship, but transforms it (e.g., T-21.III.6:1-4). In other words, we do not fire our spouses or partners because they are not students of *A Course in Miracles!* Yet this does not necessarily mean we remain in the relationship, but it is wise to be wary of the need to make external shifts, forcing change on ourselves or others. The Holy Spirit transforms the special relationship by shifting its purpose, not necessarily its form: what we made to harm He now uses to heal—*the special function.*

Again, the life you judge to be an horrendous failure can be the very means Jesus uses to lead you home. What could be holier? Your life of specialness —guilt, hate, and pain—becomes the happy path that will lead you to peace. To the extent to which you judge, attack, criticize, or languish in guilt, you prevent yourself from achieving that goal. This does not mean that your life itself is holy, but it also does not mean it is unholy. The truth is that your life is nothing, for it is its purpose that provides all meaning—the *content,* not the *form.* Since everyone comes into this world with built-in limitations as the choice over the unlimited nature of God's Love, we all are insane.

Moreover, as there is no hierarchy of illusions, there can be no hierarchy of limitations or insanity. Anyone who believes he or she is here is sick and obviously limited. Accepting that premise means you will not be tempted to use suffering—yours or another's—to prove the reality of the separation. Even if you do, you will at least recognize your motives. The ego would have you take sides and judge hierarchically, but Jesus asks you to see your judgments as a classroom, the curriculum from which he will teach that everyone is the same in content.

To be sure, in the world of dreams there are degrees. Some people are more vicious or nicer than others; some are farther up the spiritual ladder. However, when you stand outside the dream, above the battleground, you realize there is no hierarchy. Whether you are on the bottom or top rungs of the ladder, you are still on an illusion. And so there is no order within the wrong-minded and right-minded thought systems: the ego is 100 percent hate; the Holy Spirit 100 percent love. It is our going back and forth between the two that provides the temporal experience of gradation and process. Because we fragmented from the same thought, everyone has the same split mind: a thought of hate and guilt, a thought of forgiveness and love, and the power to choose between them. This provides a radically different view of yourself and everyone else, as there is no judgment inherent in this vision; no seeking to prove others wrong. They may indeed be wrong in form, but their right minds never are. Since wrongness has no hierarchy, what is the problem?

Any time we indulge in comparison, we listen to the ego. At the beginning we made the original comparison: our love is better than God's, for it recognizes our individuality, specialness, and uniqueness, which God's Love does not. Our Creator, however, did not even know about our love, because love makes no comparisons (T-24.II.1:1; W-pI.195.4:2). This ideal of making no comparisons is the goal of our journey. Since God does not know about anything outside Him—there *is* nothing outside Him—He knows nothing at all about the dream. Jesus, who represents the part of the fragmented Sonship that has awakened, knows that nothing happened as well. He makes no comparisons between his brothers because he recognizes our joint insanity and sanity. Jesus' function is to help us see this inherent equality within the Sonship, so that we would choose as he did to look at the insanity of separation and withdraw our belief in it. He teaches us to regard our tendencies to compare, find fault, and make the shadows of limitations real as his means to help us realize that this is the ego's strategy to confuse us about the truth that we separated as one Son, and therefore we return as one. The implication of this teaching is that when the mind of any fragment is healed, the Sonship as a whole is healed: the mind of God's Son is one.

This oneness is not understandable from the battleground, but only from above it, the source of this course. Its content—the loving wisdom that comes through every page—is outside the dream, yet is expressed within it in symbols we can accept, understand, and learn from. Jesus invites us to this place of peace above the battleground where together we can look on the world from the perspective that everyone here is insane and limited—being born, taking a breath, simply being in a body, are expressive of the inherent limitation of the insanity of separation. Why should we emphasize a particular form of limitation, when we share the one thought that contains them all?

This approach helps us become more tolerant, gentle, and understanding, for we see everyone's pain and can never judge those we understand. The pain behind their actions calls for kindness, not attack. Recall the lesson "I will be still an instant and go home" (W-pI.182). The first part speaks movingly of how this world is not our home, and how we try to cover up the agony of wandering in a world in which we do not belong, with no knowledge of how to get home. Imagine the terror of a little child who loses its parents in a crowd. This is *our* terror, for we all have gotten lost in the crowd of this physical world, and believe we have lost our Parent or Source. We do not hear the Voice that calls to us, because in an insanely perverse way we like being lost and on our own. We especially like that it was not our fault—others are responsible for our state: *they* lost *us*. Whose heart would not go out in compassionate kindness to such painful insanity, if only it is heard?

Our new compassion, born of Jesus' love, kindly embraces everyone who "wanders in this world uncertain, lonely, and in constant fear" (T-31.VIII.7:1). This includes all God's separated Sons, who desperately—

albeit futilely—attempt to find some certainty or hope here. They establish relationships with other bodies so the loneliness will be gone, yet the underlying fear is that none of this will work and God will yet find them and strike them dead. Religions evolved as a way to cover the pain of this loneliness—in fact, every *ism* has arisen in our world to cover this pain. When we lift ourselves above the battleground and look with Jesus, however, our hearts inevitably embrace everyone, because we hear the universal cry of suffering. The world's most fiendish villain is still crying out: "Please show me I am wrong. Please show me there is another way."

What is most important, then, is that we look differently on our lives, not through the eyes of judgment but from the perspective of a classroom in which we want to learn the lessons Jesus would teach, reclaiming our special function of forgiveness—for our salvation and that of the world.

We now turn to excerpts from the section called "The Special Function," and in our discussion focus on the specific application of the special function of forgiveness to our limitations and those of others. We begin with paragraph 4:

(T-25.VI.4:1) Such is the Holy Spirit's kind perception of specialness; His use of what you made, to heal instead of harm.

We all have a special relationship with our limitations, since these have been the defining elements in our lives—what we have striven to overcome, compensate for, and embrace as evidence for our victimized and sinless selves. We have cherished our special faults and imperfections, for they have reinforced our self-concepts of innocence, but always at the expense of others. Yet the Holy Spirit does not undo this specialness, nor seek to destroy or punish it. Rather, His kind gentleness uses it as a teaching aid to lead us home.

(4:2) To each He gives a special function in salvation he alone can fill a part for only him.

We can understand our special function as the way in which we learn to forgive our limitations—different functions in form, but with the same content of forgiveness. Each of us traverses a different highway on our journey, though our shift in purpose from guilt to forgiveness unites us along the way. We learn to practice with our specific limitations, as well as those we perceive in others, and gradually generalize our experience so that what we learn with one we learn for all—there is no hierarchy of limitations. We alone are responsible for our unhappiness, and our only need— shared with everyone—is to awaken from the ego's dream of guilt and failure. The sole answer to that need is forgiveness; the sole Teacher to learn it from is the Holy Spirit.

Once we learn we are forgiven, these limitations no longer serve the ego's purpose of protecting us from the mind's sin. This was accomplished by projection, wherein our perceived faults and failures were seen in others, holding them responsible for our unhappiness. Recognizing that the ego's tale of sin was made up, we now realize that nothing separated us from the Love of God, which has always been with us. Our imperfect lives thus no longer need to express the imperfect thought of separation, and consequently disappear "into the nothingness from which [they] came" (M-13.1:2), along with the ego's thought system of judgment and limitation.

(4:3) Nor is the plan complete until he finds his special function, and fulfills the part assigned to him, to make himself complete within a world where incompletion rules.

This is an incomplete, imperfect, and limited world, since it came from an incomplete, imperfect, and limited thought—*ideas leave not their source*. Indeed, how can a world that was made as an attack on God, as the workbook tells us (W-pII.3.2:1), be anything but incomplete, imperfect, and limited, not to mention hateful, sorrowful, lonely, and moribund? However, within that world we can yet be complete because we exist as a mind and not a body. We remember our completion by joining with the Voice that speaks for it, instead of with the voice that speaks for lack, and then makes us believe that joining with its specialness constitutes completion.

The part assigned *to* me was assigned *by* me. When I made up my script of limitations and incompletion, I assigned myself the role of being victimized by them, including those whom I ultimately held to be responsible for them. In asking Jesus for help, I keep the same script of limitations, but with a different purpose. Instead of seeing myself as a victim, I see myself as one who is learning to forgive, remembering that my completion lies within my right mind, independent of the body and the wrong-minded thought system that made it.

(5:1) Here, where the laws of God do not prevail in perfect form, can he yet do *one* perfect thing and make *one* perfect choice.

The "*one* perfect thing" is to forgive, which fulfils our special function; the "*one* perfect choice" is to choose the Holy Spirit as our Teacher. Indeed, the only perfect thing we can do here is forgive. We cannot have a perfect body, relationship, job—a perfect anything; nor can we live in a perfect world that was made *not* to be perfect. We cannot change what the world is, but we can change the purpose we give to it.

The perfect thing to do in the world is to perceive its imperfection without judgment. *That* we can learn to do—*perfectly.*

(5:2) And by this act of special faithfulness to one perceived as other than himself, he learns the gift was given to himself, and so they must be one.

The "act of special faithfulness" is geared towards our special love or hate partners, whom we perceive as different from us. In the context of the subject of this book we can liken this perception to a difference of limitations. The way we express our special function is to take the special relationship—our perception of others as different, not just in form but in content— and begin to understand through our new Teacher that we are wrong in our perception, and the truth is that we are all alike—in limitation *and* in limitlessness. Our forms may differ radically, but we come to learn that we are on the same battleground—taking different positions and choosing different weapons, yet being the same. That is Jesus' point here: the forgiveness I offer you I must offer to myself because we are one—no *you* outside my mind, no *me* as a body outside my mind. In the text, Jesus asks us:

> What if you recognized this world is an hallucination? What if you really understood you made it up? What if you realized that those who

78

seem to walk about in it, to sin and die, attack and murder and destroy themselves, are wholly unreal? Could you have faith in what you see, if you accepted this? (T-20.VIII.7:3-6)

If we could accept this truth about the illusion, the world of limitation would not upset us. We would not attack or judge it, which makes us part of the very problem we are attempting to solve. This is the reason problems are never truly solved here, for the people attempting to solve them, no matter how well-intentioned, end up as aspects of the problem. They see the limitation, imperfection, and problem as real, and do not recognize their source in themselves. Healing, let alone its kindness, totally eludes them.

(5:5) Forgiveness is for all.

This principle is the key to *A Course in Miracles*—our need to forgive *all* aspects of the separated Sonship, without exception. However, we can also apply it to the need to forgive *all* our perceived limitations, without exception. Not one of the ego's spots of darkness can be excluded from Jesus' healing and gentle kindness. In the text's final vision, Jesus says: "Not one spot of darkness still remains to hide the face of Christ from anyone" (T-31.VIII.12:5). *Not one spot of darkness!* If I exclude one darkened limitation in myself or others, I am choosing to retain a darkened thought of guilt—the original limitation. Jesus' vision must be extended to all aspects of the illusion, which is what makes his course so difficult. Indeed, Jesus tells us that in order to learn it, we must question every value that we hold (T-24.in.2:1), and these must include the values—negative or positive—we have placed on the ego's limitations, for not one can be more or less significant than any other: there is no hierarchy of illusions. Yet we need not feel guilty because we have accorded these values to the ego's limitations. We would not be here if we had not been so inclined, and as Jesus translates specialness from sin to salvation, its content has been gently forgiven.

(5:6-8) But when it rests on all it is complete, and every function of this world completed with it. Then is time no more. Yet while in time, there is still much to do.

Though this passage offers a vision of the journey's end, when limitations are gone, we should not dwell on it because we are not yet ready, still believing we live in time—the work of forgiveness remains for us to do. When one person has fulfilled his function of total forgiveness of limitations, it is fulfilled for all, since minds are one. Nonetheless, the fragments that still believe they are here have yet to make that choice. Hence, those who have made that decision are helpful to those who have not, reminding them of the choice they, too, can make.

(5:9-11) And each must do what is allotted him, for on his part does all the plan depend. He *has* a special part in time for so he chose, and choosing it, he made it for himself. His wish was not denied but changed in form, to let it serve his brother and himself, and thus become a means to save instead of lose.

The special limitations we chose become the Holy Spirit's means for changing the mind's content or purpose, the meaning of the above words "changed in form." We are not asked to let the limitation go, but simply to accept its form with the kind purpose of forgiveness that will return us home. The limitation or defect that represented to us the belief in sin and guilt —the loss of our innocence—becomes the means of our salvation. The limitation we made to harm is now a way of saving us from our mistaken choice. The ego's purpose of specialness, on the other hand, is to keep us as far away from home as possible; i.e., in the harsh world of limited and mindless bodies.

It is essential that we accept our lives as they are. This is not meant simplistically, however, in that we are never to make external changes. Rather, it means that we should not make external changes for the wrong reason, because that always reflects some aspect of specialness. Before we change our lives— seeking to better ourselves, for example—we want to be as free as possible of the cruel burdens of guilt we placed upon this life. This would enable the healing love within to flow through the mind, and whatever we then do or say would be helpful for us and everyone else. As always, we are not speaking of behavior, but the kind forgiveness that allows behavior to reflect love instead of hate.

(6:1-3) Salvation is no more than a reminder this world is not your home. Its laws are not imposed on you, its values are not yours. And nothing that you think you see in it is really there at all.

If this world of limitation is not our home, why fix it? Why not do what Jesus asks so that we can find our real home, instead of seeking to remedy a limitation that is not who we are? Jesus thus gently informs us we are insane: seeing what is not there, thinking what is not true. The world does not impose its laws of limitation on us because the world does not exist, and how can the non-existent affect us? We impose our wish for limitation and lack on the world so it will seem to impose them on us, allowing us to conveniently forget *we* have done it. We choose our limitations, as we have chosen to live under the ego's laws. We made the original choice because the ego told us it would help solidify our individual identity. The point, therefore, is not to change the limitation, but to change the purpose we had given it. This means changing to the teacher who will show us how to approach these limitations and those of others with kindness and understanding, rather than attack and judgment. Once again, this is not about changing the external form of the limitation, but changing our minds about the form. The text reminds us of this crucial distinction: "Therefore, seek not to change the world, but choose to change your mind about the world" (T-21.in.1:7).

(6:6-8) The specialness he chose to hurt himself did God appoint to be the means for his salvation, from the very instant that the choice was made. His special sin was made his special grace. His special hate became his special love.

We do not change anything external, only the way we perceive what *seems* to be external—shifting from the eyes of judgment to vision, specialness to forgiveness. Thus Jesus teaches that we should not be upset by our shadows of limitation, for we came to undo them. When we become judgmental, guilty, murderous, or excited, we make the shadows real. Our right-minded purpose, however, is to reverse the ego's reason for our coming, so that the tiny, mad road into insanity becomes nothing more than a detour that will as surely lead us home as will traversing a straight line. One takes longer, but we are only speaking of time, which is inherently unreal. There is no need to pressure ourselves or others, or seek to impose guilt. And so we learn the kind gentleness of patience that reflects remembering to laugh at the ego's tiny, mad idea of separation and limitation.

(7:1-3) The Holy Spirit needs your special function, that His may be fulfilled. Think not you lack a special value here. You wanted it, and it is given you.

We wanted the special value the ego places on limitation and we received it. God would not accord our limitation any value, so we took it upon ourselves to make it our own. The Holy Spirit takes what we made and gives it an authentic value as our special function. The special relationship, with all its imperfections, will remind us of the original special relationship our minds chose by forging an alliance with the ego. By focusing on the mind instead of the body, we are able to correct this mistaken choice and have the special value we wanted, but with a different purpose.

(7:4-5) All that you made can serve salvation easily and well. The Son of God can make no choice the Holy Spirit cannot employ on his behalf, and not against himself.

This is the heart of *A Course in Miracles*. We do not hate the limited world or body. We embrace them, not because they are wonderful in and of themselves, but because their imperfections can serve a holy function as we learn from our mistakes. Yet we cannot learn if we judge, as judging merely plunges us into guilt and ensures that nothing will change. If, however, we use our errors as the means of helping us understand the mind's insane thinking, everything will change, for our limited life will now have the meaning of forgiveness.

(7:6) Only in darkness does your specialness appear to be attack.

When you are on the battleground and become aware of the gruesome aspects of specialness— viciousness, hatred, and pain—it is difficult not to feel the hurtful effects of being a limited self. The guilt inherent in such a self-concept drives us ever deeper into special relationships, the ego's insane attempt to escape guilt. However, it is only within the darkness of guilt, born of limitation, that our relationship appears as an attack.

(7:7) In light, you see it as your special function in the plan to save the Son of God from all attack, and let him understand that he is safe, as he has always been, and will remain in time and in eternity alike.

We see this idea expressed in "The Judgment of the Holy Spirit," where Jesus explains that attack is an expression of fear, and fear a call for the love that has been denied (T-12.I). Through the eyes of guilt, specialness *is* an attack; through the eyes of forgiveness —Christ's vision—it is a way to learn the holy instant's lessons that lead us home. Once again, the road of limitation the ego led us down becomes the contours of the road that will lead us back.

To repeat, we are not asked in *A Course in Miracles* to deny the obvious limitations of life in the body—personally or collectively. Our life is a classroom, and by dismissing what is going on by glibly uttering "This is all an illusion and I am going to ignore it," we deny Jesus the only means in the universe he can use to help us. This, of course, is precisely why we deny it: our egos do not want the help. To pretend we are not children of our families or citizens of the world, thereby asserting it does not matter what goes on around us, is to fall prey to denial. Try not to forget that our lives of limitations are classrooms that afford Jesus the opportunity to help us— our special sin was made our special grace; our special hate became our special love. If we deny our belief that limitation is a sin, it cannot be turned into grace; if we deny it is hate, it cannot be turned into love; if we deny it was a mistake, it cannot be corrected by forgiveness.

As our kind teacher, Jesus says to us: "Let me help you look at your world through my eyes, and you will see everything differently." He teaches us that everyone calls for help. *Everyone*—not some, not just the people we like. Take any conflict and talk to people about both sides of the conflict—whether international or personal—and invariably you will get different perceptions of what is good and what is evil. The truth is that within the dream everyone is good, everyone is evil, everyone is insane. The sane and the good do not come here, but stay home with Sanity and Goodness. Observe your tendency to exclude or make exceptions. *The* characteristic of special relationships is exclusivity, whereas *the* characteristic of holy relationships is inclusivity. Since specialness excludes, it always involves comparisons. The holy relationship, which shifts to the Holy Spirit as Teacher, includes everyone, without exception. And this is the kindness that heals the belief in separation and limitation.

(7:8-10) This is the function given you for your brother. Take it gently, then, from your brother's hand, and let salvation be perfectly fulfilled in you. Do this *one* thing, that everything be given you.

If we want happiness and peace, freedom from guilt, fear and pain, we need do this *one* thing: fulfill the special function of forgiving our limitations. We ask the Holy Spirit's help to perceive our special love or hate partners differently—the projected objects of our failings—which means no longer seeing differences. It is helpful to know how difficult this is to do. It may be easier with some relationships than with others, but it is extremely tempting to make differences important. Returning to Plato's Allegory of the Cave, it is difficult to see that there is something beyond the shadows, because we do not want to be freed from the cave—the ego's prison of separation, specialness, and limitation that is the home of our self.

We are sped along the journey by being aware of our resistance to learning the simple truth. We do not have to pretend we are spiritually advanced, but we need to accept how quickly we revert to making judgments; how quickly we identify with our limitations or someone else's; how quickly we attack, criticize, and judge, as if limitations made a difference; how easily we justify our thoughts and acts of unkindness. Recall that simply coming into this world as a body is a limitation. *That* makes a difference, because it is the difference between the ego's limitation and God's unlimited Love—the only difference that is important. All else exists within the same illusion, and so personal and specific limitations are irrelevant. How could an illusion make any difference to the peace of God? If God does not see our limitations, why should we, unless we think we know better than He? Needless to say, that was the mistake we fell into at the beginning, saying God's perfect Love and Oneness were not enough, and making a world in which we proclaimed our superiority to God—limitation having triumphed over the limitless.

Looking at history, for instance, is helpful because it shows us what a terrible mess we have made of things—past as well as present. This can stimulate us to realize, in a much larger context, the mess that is the world. We are naïve if we think this situation is due to one person or group, although in one sense it *can* be attributed to one person and group: the one Son of God and the Sonship in its separated state. We *all* made a mess when we believed we could leave home and be happy. Why, then, should we try to judge among differences? A mess is a mess is a mess! Since no one is home, everyone's life is the same in content. Jesus refers to the body and ego self as travesties and parodies of God's creation (T-24.VII.10:9; 1:11); shabby substitutes for the glorious Self of Christ that God created (T-16.IV.8:4). Once we are embedded in the ego's shabby thought system, what difference does the form make? That is why judging among limitations is insane, for the only sane judgment is that limitations are equally insane, without exception.

And so we evoke the healing power of kindness to comfort those in pain, which embraces all the Sonship, including ourselves. Our task now is only to demonstrate to others the joy of releasing investment in limitations, which allows the limitless Love of the Holy Spirit to flow through us, embracing the limited Sons in the peace that comes from the Unlimited. This is the subject of the concluding chapter.

5. Demonstrating Forgiveness

Our discussion of Jesus' instruction that we be not upset by shadows, for that is why we came, was a means of demonstrating that the world is a classroom in which we learn. To complete the discussion, we need add that it is also a classroom in which we teach —namely that we have fulfilled our special function and are forgiven, freeing us to be instruments of the Holy Spirit's Love. Similarly, we are told in the clarification of terms that just as Jesus was the manifestation of the Holy Spirit, he asks that we be his manifestation as well (C-6.5:1-4). In the lovely Introduction to the fifth review in the workbook, he tells us:

> For this alone I need; that you will hear the words
> I speak, and give them to the world. You are my
> voice, my eyes, my feet, my hands through which
> I save the world (W-pI.rvV.9:2-3).

In this final chapter, we discuss how we become Jesus' manifestation and, specifically, how our limitations serve as the means of our teaching. We begin by looking at the third paragraph in "Can God Be Reached Directly?" (M-26) from the teacher's manual:

(M-26.3:7) All worldly states must be illusory.

Reflect for a moment on the word *All*—"All worldly states must be illusory." We are familiar by now with the idea that there is no hierarchy of limitations, for all things are illusory. This includes *A Course in Miracles*, Jesus, and each of us. Since nothing here is in a state of perfect Oneness, nothing here can be of God and therefore cannot be real. The only important distinction in the world of illusion is between wrong-minded and right-minded illusions; the former reinforce separation, while the latter undo it. That is the only meaningful distinction one can make in the post-separation state, and why it is senseless to judge among various *forms* of limitations, seeing some as more or less significant than others.

(3:8) If God were reached directly in sustained awareness, the body would not be long maintained.

If you experienced total Oneness with God, there would no longer be a split mind and the body would simply disappear.

(3:9) Those who have laid the body down merely to extend their helpfulness to those remaining behind are few indeed.

This includes someone like Jesus. He referred to this state in paragraph 2 as "Teachers of teachers," and he also speaks of it in the *Psychotherapy* pamphlet in terms of the ideal psychotherapist, one who has attained the real world (P-2.III.3:7–4:4). Those who have transcended all limitation are few indeed and we need not dwell upon them, but only on the process of forgiveness that will bring us to their state of unlimited helpfulness.

(3:10) And they need helpers who are still in bondage and still asleep, so that by their awakening can God's Voice be heard.

This statement is the essence of Jesus' teaching, paralleling his earlier description of God's advanced teachers, as distinguished from those who are at the bottom of the ladder, still believing they are bodies. The advanced teachers incorporate the ten characteristics Jesus explained earlier (M-4) and remain within the ego world; but they are far enough along to have God's Voice speak through them. It is in this context, then, that Jesus says:

(4:1-5) Do not despair, then, because of limitations. It is your function to escape from them, but not to be without them. If you would be heard by those who suffer, you must speak their language. If you would be a savior, you must understand what needs to be escaped. Salvation is not theoretical.

This is the right-minded view of our limitations, once we have purified them of the guilt and hate that produced them. The ego had us come here to maintain these limitations in order to be able to justify blaming others for our unhappiness and misfortune. Of utmost importance is recognizing that as we learn our lessons and fulfill our special function, these limitations do not necessarily go away. The point is that we learn not to be upset or concerned if they remain, for it is not our function to be without imperfections, but to escape the terrible burden of guilt we placed upon ourselves for having them. It is in this vein that one could understand highly advanced people like Ramakrishna and Ramana Maharshi succumbing to cancer—a wonderful lesson on how one can have a fatal disease, and still keep one's equanimity. In other words, the body may be ill, but the mind retains its perfect health.

We need our limitations because that is part of what keeps us here, and they become the means for others to relate to us as well. It is extremely difficult to relate to a Jesus, whose self merely appears to be here. We need people who look like us, have similar problems and limitations, but are not like us in the sense that they listen to a different voice. The beginning of Lesson 155 says of God's teachers (although that term is not used there) that they look like everyone else, but they smile more frequently and their foreheads are serene (W-pI.155.1:2-3). That is how they stand out, not by how they speak, eat, or dress, but because love, peace, and gentle kindness shine through their limited and imperfect selves.

Note the words: "If you would be heard by those who suffer, you must speak their language." Regrettably, students of *A Course in Miracles*, under the guise of being holy, spiritual, and metaphysically correct, often stop acting human. They even cease speaking the language of other people. There are some, for example, who attend funerals with big smiles on their faces, wearing bright clothes and coming to celebrate that nothing happened. All this while everyone else is appropriately sad. Yet these "holy" students are smiling and happy because they know, metaphysically, that death is nothing. Sadly, however, they have separated themselves from the people they are purporting to love and help. They but pretend to have transcended their limitations when it is obvious, in view of their behavior, that they have transcended nothing. There are, unfortunately, many similar examples that could be cited.*

As a review of our previous discussion, we can note the importance of this passage in reminding us that we not despair because of limitations, for it is all right to have a limited self. Yet now our imperfections can serve the different purpose of communicating in a language people can accept and understand. We do not attempt to be different—holier– or more spiritual-than-thou—but rather let the love extend through us

---

* For further discussion of this issue, see *Releasing Judgment,* Volume One of *The Healing Power of Kindness*.

in whatever way is helpful. That is why it is so important to remember that this is a course in *content* and not *form*. Our task is merely to ask for help to remove the blocks to the awareness of love's content. In different ways throughout the text, Jesus says that our task is to choose the miracle, salvation, or holiness. Their extension through us is not our responsibility, which is but to let love extend by making room for it, without concern for the form its extension takes in the world.

The danger in any non-dualism is that people will use it as a defense against dealing with their egos, one of the most serious mistakes students of *A Course in Miracles* can make, wherein the idea that the world is illusory is used as a reason not to deal with it. Everything—most especially difficult relationships—is brushed aside as an illusion, even though Jesus urges us not to deny our experiences and reject the very limitations he can use to lead us to the limitless. He asks us only to deny the ego's interpretation of our relationships and situations.

The story of Helen Schucman, William Thetford, and the scribing of *A Course in Miracles* reflects this point of Jesus using our limitations. The Course did not come to a holy nun buried in a convent in the middle of the desert, but to two psychologists locked in a bitter struggle with each other, and with everyone else in a medical center—Columbia-Presbyterian—that is among the greatest symbols of the ego's thought system of competition and hate, in a city that is the world's center for specialness and greed. That world of limitation was the Course's manger. Moreover, at the time Helen was taking down the Course, she and Bill were at their busiest, and *A Course in Miracles* had to be fit into their very hectic professional lives of applying for grants, editing journals, writing papers, running a department, and dealing with relationship issues on all levels, most especially with each other.

Herein lies an important message: To be sure, limitations differ widely among the Sonship, as does everyone's pathway home. However, while some may indeed be guided not to be involved in the world, these would be rare instances. In general, *A Course in Miracles* is for those living normal lives, indistinguishable from any other, and who are not asked to live differently except to forgive—not changing the *forms* of their limitations, but their underlying *content* or purpose.

Turn now to "What Is the Role of Words in Healing?" (M-21), which begins by defining words as illusions, but now with a different purpose:

(M-21.1:7) God does not understand words, for they were made by separated minds to keep them in the illusion of separation.

In that sense, words are not seen in a positive light for they were made as an attack on God. They keep us separate from each other and "are but symbols of symbols.... twice removed from reality" (1:9-10), which, by the way, comes from Plato's *Republic*. Words are symbols of a concept, and the concept represents reality. For example, the reality is God's Love, about which we have a concept, and then we use words to describe it. However, the words and concept are *not* the Love.

Nonetheless, in paragraph 4, Jesus says:

(4:1-2) Is the teacher of God, then, to avoid the use of words in his teaching? No, indeed!

In effect, Jesus is warning us not to be "metaphysically correct," because to do so would be an attack. The content common to everyone is the belief in separation, the foundation for all limitations and the core of all problems. We believe we are separate from God and from each other, for which our guilt holds us responsible. If, then, the problem is believing separation is real, the answer is an experience of our joining. If I use words to judge and criticize you from a position of spiritual advancement, however, I am teaching and reinforcing the very thing that is your problem. This means it is my problem, too, and I am using words to keep us separate. However, even though words were made to keep the separation alive, they can now serve a different purpose:

(4:3) There are many who must be reached through words, being as yet unable to hear in silence.

Most people are afraid of silence because the ego says that God will get us when we are quiet and our defenses are down. Interestingly, fundamentalist Christians believe the devil will get them if their minds are quiet, which is why they do not meditate. These fears, however, are really of the guilt that would arise in the silence, and why the ego made a noisy thought system—sin and guilt are not quiet; neither is the fear of God's murderous wrath. Make no mistake, the ego's is not the still, small Voice of the Holy Spirit, but a cacophony of raucous shrieks, which it covers with a noise-filled world that includes our noisy bodies. Fearing silence, we fear physical quiet, which symbolizes the mind's quiet in which the still, small Voice can be heard. Thus the Holy Spirit's soft and gentle message is drowned out by the harsh sounds of hate, suffering, and death, which in turn are covered by the body and its world.

Uneasy with silence, people need words, which means that in our right mind words are accorded a different purpose. Rather than using words to separate, we use them to demonstrate that the separation from God never happened, and therefore the separation between brothers never happened. If you are sane and I am not, sanity would take the form of love coming through in ways I would experience without fear. That is the meaning of this helpful passage in Chapter 2:

> The value of the Atonement does not lie in the manner in which it is expressed. In fact, if it is used truly, it will inevitably be expressed in whatever way is most helpful to the receiver. This means that a miracle, to attain its full efficacy, must be expressed in a language that the recipient can understand without fear (T-2.IV.5:1-3).

This means that you will do and say whatever I would not experience as fearful, regardless of the form. There is a wonderful story of Beethoven that nicely illustrates the primacy of *content* and the subordinate place of *form*. When a close friend of the Master was devastated by the death of her last child, he invited her to come to him. On her arrival he sat down at the piano and said: "We will now talk to each other in tones." He then played for over an hour, without saying a word, and she later remarked to a friend: "He told me everything, and at last brought me comfort."

In the *Psychotherapy* pamphlet, Jesus cautions his therapists to listen truly to their patients, for they will reveal all that they need, if they are but listened to (P-3.I.2:1-7). As always, Jesus is speaking of *content*, not *form*. *Listen.* Do not presume to know what you should say or do as an intervention with this person, despite what professional textbooks or training programs tell you. There is no way you could know. *Listen.* When you are quiet, the Holy Spirit will speak through you, ensuring that whatever you say will be gentle, loving, kind, and helpful. Words will now assume a different meaning because they have come from a different Source, fulfilling a different purpose —the healing power of kindness has come to replace the attack of separation.

(4:4) The teacher of God must, however, learn to use words in a new way.

The old way is the ego telling me what to say, such as in my thinking I know what you require in this situation: a good, healthy dose of *A Course in Miracles*! Rather than demonstrate to you the Course's kind and gentle truth, I take its truth and hit you over the head with it, confusing *form* with *content*. The Course, after all, is nothing more than a set of symbols that mean nothing if you do not let them connect you to their source: the Love of God. Yes, you want to teach people that *A Course in Miracles* is true, but what makes it true is the non-ego love that inspired it. The goal is to be a manifestation of that love as it is demonstrated through you. You need not know what to say or do; only to be clear that you want yourself out of the way—an expression of the little willingness. To say it differently, what matters is not what you say, but Who says it through you, for the content of God's Love is the teacher.

You may recall that in the beginning of the manual, Jesus states that to teach is to demonstrate (M-in.2), and we demonstrate one of two thought systems—the Holy Spirit or the ego. Whether I am teaching arithmetic, nuclear physics, *A Course in Miracles*, or plumbing is irrelevant. I am teaching one of two thought systems in *content*. What you learn from me is not what I say on the level of words, which is ultimately irrelevant, but the thought systems of fear, guilt, and separation, or healing, forgiveness, and love. Obviously, I will be appropriate to the situation —if you come to me to learn arithmetic, I am not going to teach you nuclear physics. That would hardly be loving. Yet there are two ways of teaching arithmetic: making students feel demeaned or worthwhile. In both cases the students may end up learning how to add two and two. However, one will be an experience of guilt and shame, and the other an experience of acceptance and respect. As Jesus says to us: "Teach not that I died in vain; teach rather that I did not die by demonstrating that I live in you" (T-11.VI.7:3-4). We teach the validity of his thought system of resurrection —awakening from the dream of death—by practicing it. Again, we demonstrate it to a world of illusion through our limitations—the condition in which people think they live (T-25.I.7:4).

Forgiveness is the key idea in awakening from the dream of death—our understanding that the separation never happened. I cannot demonstrate this principle of the Atonement unless I believe it, which means I first have to undo my disbelief—a thought system of judgment and specialness. If I need to be seen as holy, wise, brilliant, kind, and loving, I am going to be teaching need, not its end. I have to be aware of my own neediness in situations, and once aware, I can truly ask for help—not in terms of what I should teach or say, but in getting my ego thought system out of the way. I need not be ego free—i.e., free of limitations—but I do need the *willingness* to be ego free.

In another message to Helen, Jesus said not to ask him what she should say to someone, even though that would seem to be a good thing: "Here is a person needing help, Jesus; what should I say?" The essence of his response was: "Don't ask me what to say, but rather ask for help to look through the eyes of peace and not judgment."* Once the judgment is removed, whatever is said will inevitably be helpful because it will have come from a place of non-separation. When one has joined with Jesus, his love will flow naturally from that union and will manifest in words and behavior. To restate this important caution about *form* and *content*, what I say to you today may not be what I would say to you tomorrow. If I am a therapist, what I say to a patient at two o'clock may be the opposite of what I would say to a different patient at four o'clock. The form does not matter; it may even be quite inconsistent. That is why the second characteristic of God's teachers—*honesty*—is defined as "consistency": what you say and do is consistent with what you think (M-4.II). If you think love, your behavior will be consistent with the thought, which might guide you to say something that is helpful today, but five minutes or five months from now may guide you to say the exact opposite in words, though the loving *content* would remain the same.

Sometimes when I have given advice to a person, I find that he or she has subsequently told others that they should do the same thing. The person meant well, but what was said for one to express a *content* of love may be totally unhelpful in *form* for another. This

---

* See *Absence from Felicity*, p. 381.

mistake occurs because people, to make the point one more time, tend to confuse form and content. This is a key aspect in the practice of *A Course in Miracles*, and why Jesus points out that the special relationship is a "triumph of form over content" (T-16.V.12:1-4)— an error made by every formal religion. When there are sacred people, rituals, customs, objects, places, and words, they end up reflecting this triumph of hate and fear. When you identify with the content of love, however, the form is automatically kind and gentle. Its expression in form may be inconsistent, but the content is one, and limitations have been kindly transformed by love into helpfulness. At this point, Jesus asks us to use our limitations as a way to heal the mind, allowing his healing love to work through our limited selves and reach other limited selves. We are then not perceived as special or unique, but as one of the Sonship; yet with a love and wisdom that people recognize make us different, for we no longer seek to fulfill the personal needs that reinforce separate interests.

(4:5-6) Gradually, he learns how to let his words be chosen for him by ceasing to decide for himself what he will say. This process is merely a special case of the lesson in the workbook that says, "I will step back and let Him lead the way."

Stepping back means withdrawing from the ego. I do not pretend it is not there, but I step back from my identification with it, bringing the darkness of the ego's illusions to the light of the Holy Spirit's truth. When I identify with the Holy Spirit and His thought system of inclusion, things do not necessarily change externally; what changes is the purpose given them. As I withdraw my judgments of limitation and imperfection—mine and others—I allow the Holy Spirit to interpret them for me. His loving kindness enables me to forgive myself, which opens the way for Him to teach others the same kindness through me. What before had been a curse has become a blessing.

(4:7-9) The teacher of God accepts the words which are offered him, and gives as he receives. He does not control the direction of his speaking. He listens and hears and speaks.

I listen to the Holy Spirit's message of forgiveness instead of the ego's tale of guilt, allowing His words of love to be mine, as did Helen when she took down *A Course in Miracles*, stepping back from her ego to let Jesus lead the way. Since he was a symbol of God's Love for her, she joined with that love by *not* joining with the ego. Her mind was quiet, enabling her to "hear" his voice, "listening" to his message of love as the words inevitably flowed through her. In this sense everyone channels, for we all hear an inner voice—there is no outer one. The only question is which voice will we listen to. That is why the focus of *A Course in Miracles* is on becoming aware of the ego's investment in separation and its need for specialness, which we bring to Jesus for healing.

Jesus repeatedly asked Helen to exchange the gifts of fear for the gifts of God, saying in so many words:[*] "I cannot give you my love until you first give me your fear. In effect, you have only one hand, and if it is filled with guilt, fear, and specialness, there is no room for love. I cannot take guilt from you, and so you must look at it with me so I may teach you what it is, where it comes from, why you chose it, and what you have lost in your wrong-minded decision. Thus you will be motivated to give it to me, and when you do, your empty hand will be filled with the Love of God."

What speeds you on this detour home is asking for help whenever you become aware that you are making real some difference between you and another. Any thought you have that establishes a difference between you must be of the ego—a red flag you cannot miss if you are paying attention. However, try not to dwell on it, and above all, try not to justify, rationalize, or

---

[*] See, for example, *The Gifts of God*, pp. 118-19.

defend it. Simply say: "Obviously I must be in the ego's thought system of separation because I am not making a judgment about someone that I am willing to make about everyone, including myself." To underscore the principle discussed earlier, any thought you have that you would not apply to everyone in the Sonship must be of the ego. You do not have to analyze or seek to understand the judgment, but recognize what it is and how it cancels out the underlying thought that views everyone as having the same needs, interests, and goals.

As students of *A Course in Miracles,* we are asked first to learn and practice its teachings. Once we do, the love we have made room for will work through us. Whenever you feel you have important work to do in this world—e.g., a specific function Jesus has given you—you should smile knowingly and gently, realizing your ego has done it again. Your only function is to forgive. Whenever you think there is something else you are supposed to do, run as quickly as you can away from yourself. If someone tells you of your function, run even faster, because they will be wanting something from you. No one has any important work they are supposed to do that differs from anyone else's. It would make no sense to think otherwise about a world that does not exist. Our only important work is to change the mind that thinks there is a world, let alone something important that needs to be done within it.

This does not mean, however, that you do not do things here—our bodies would not long exist if they did not function. The question is, however, *who* is the agent of the functioning—the ego or the Holy Spirit? You know it is your ego if you think what you are doing is important, or if what you are doing is *un*important because it is not what others do. The ego blesses either alternative, for it thrives on the comparisons of specialness. When you compare yourself with others, wherein you are important and they are not because Jesus gave you a special assignment, or you think you are the dregs of the earth because everyone else has assignments and you have nothing important to do— it is the same thing, for you see differences where there are none. An illusion dressed in blue is no different from an illusion dressed in red; an illusion dressed in importance—which is really self-importance—is no different from an illusion dressed in non-importance. Anything that makes a perception of differences real must be of the ego. The only way you should think of yourself as having an important function is to realize everyone else has an important function, too: *forgiveness*. Remember, anything that differentiates you from another must be of the ego. There is nothing else you need to know—all limitations are inherently the same in content and purpose.

5. Demonstrating Forgiveness

As Jesus asks us to do, we bring to him our misperceptions, understanding that we perceive them because we *want* to make differences real, for in this way we keep our separate and special identities. We need only be aware of how almost everything we do, say, feel, or think is separating, for it does not embrace all people as one, where we see everyone fulfilling a common need and sharing a common goal. We should not, however, judge ourselves for our limited sight, but rather look at these misperceptions and realize why we chose them. This is the true meaning of asking for help, which cannot be accomplished without understanding the Course's underlying metaphysics that the world of separation is an illusion. A clear grasp of that principle keeps us from getting caught in the special relationship in any of its forms. Spiritual specialness is the worst of these because of its sanctimonious air of holiness and importance. We never quite realize how divisive and attacking specialness is, and in this regard it is helpful to keep in mind that *A Course in Miracles* itself is an illusion. Without question it is a most helpful one, but the Course remains what it is—a collection of words and concepts. Just as people have killed themselves over the Bible, people are very close to killing each other over this course—if not physically yet, as far as I know, certainly psychologically. This would never happen if its form were not taken so seriously.

In conclusion, we should take the loving content of *A Course in Miracles* seriously, but not its form, for then we would realize that love is perfect Oneness, which includes everyone. It is essential we be aware of how much we want to cling to our limitations or the limitations of others, and our resistance to letting the ego's thought system go. What helps us ascend the ladder of forgiveness is forgiving ourselves for *not* wanting to ascend the ladder. We are hindered in our climb, not by our perceived limitations, defects, or imperfections, but by our failure to look at them through the gentle eyes of kindness that see no grounds for judgment. Thus are we freed of the barriers to the free flow of love through our limited selves, the means whereby we learn to remember the limitlessness of God's Son.

Conclusion

From Limitation to Limitlessness

As we ascend the ladder, we are blessed by having both the means and end within us. The Holy Spirit's Love is the Means that leads us to God's Love, which is the End. The darkened shadows of our limited selves, so hated and scorned—whether perceived in ourselves or projected onto others—are transformed through forgiveness into beacons of light, illuminating our journey. Christ's vision has revealed their new purpose, and what was made to represent hate and fear has become the means to take us to our home, where Love awaits us in quiet joy.

We close by reading Lesson 302. The first part is our prayer to God, echoing the prayer to ourselves that we forgive the love that needs no forgiveness, accepting the holiness that lies just beyond the belief in limitation and lack. In the lesson's second part, Jesus instructs us that God is the only truth and love our only goal. Yet this love is within us as we make our way to the Love that is our Self. It is that Love to which we return, at the same time it is that Love we experience on life's detours that leads us through limitation to the Limitless. And so we do not short-circuit our experiences in the world, but allow them to be

113

used by Love, represented by Jesus who walks with us up the ladder until we are home—limitation having dissolved into limitlessness, as God's Son returns to God's Son:

Where darkness was I look upon the light.

Father, our eyes are opening at last. Your holy world awaits us, as our sight is finally restored and we can see. We thought we suffered. But we had forgot the Son whom You created. Now we see that darkness is our own imagining, and light is there for us to look upon. Christ's vision changes darkness into light, for fear must disappear when love has come. Let me forgive Your holy world today, that I may look upon its holiness and understand it but reflects my own.

Our Love awaits us as we go to Him, and walks beside us showing us the way. He fails in nothing. He the End we seek, and He the Means by which we go to Him.

INDEX OF REFERENCES TO *A COURSE IN MIRACLES*

text

text (cont.)

workbook for students

manual for teachers

Foundation for *A Course in Miracles*®

Kenneth Wapnick received his Ph.D. in Clinical Psychology in 1968 from Adelphi University. He was a close friend and associate of Helen Schucman and William Thetford, the two people whose joining together was the immediate stimulus for the scribing of *A Course in Miracles*. Kenneth has been involved with *A Course in Miracles* since 1973, writing, teaching, and integrating its principles with his practice of psychotherapy. He is on the Executive Board of the Foundation for Inner Peace, publishers of *A Course in Miracles*.

In 1983, with his wife Gloria, he began the Foundation for *A Course in Miracles*, and in 1984 this evolved into a Teaching and Healing Center in Crompond, New York, which was quickly outgrown. In 1988 they opened the Academy and Retreat Center in upstate New York. In 1995 they began the Institute for Teaching Inner Peace through *A Course in Miracles*, an educational corporation chartered by the New York State Board of Regents. In 2001 the Foundation moved to Temecula, California. The Foundation publishes a quarterly newsletter, "The Lighthouse," which is available free of charge. The following is Kenneth and Gloria's vision of the Foundation.

In our early years of studying *A Course in Miracles*, as well as teaching and applying its principles in our respective professions of psychotherapy, and teaching and school administration, it seemed evident that this was not the simplest of thought systems to understand. This was so not only in the intellectual grasp of its teachings, but perhaps more importantly in the application of these teachings to our personal lives. Thus, it appeared to us from the beginning that the Course lent itself to teaching, parallel to the ongoing teachings of the Holy Spirit in the daily opportunities within our relationships, which are discussed in the early pages of the manual for teachers.

One day several years ago while Helen Schucman and I (Kenneth) were discussing these ideas, she shared a vision that she had had of a teaching center as a white temple with a gold cross atop it. Although it was clear that this image was symbolic, we understood it to be representative of what the teaching center was to be: a place where the person of Jesus and his message in *A Course in Miracles* would be manifest. We have sometimes seen an image of a lighthouse shining its light into the sea, calling to it those passers-by who sought it. For us, this light is the Course's teaching of forgiveness, which we would hope to share with those who are drawn to the Foundation's form of teaching and its vision of *A Course in Miracles*.

This vision entails the belief that Jesus gave the Course at this particular time in this particular form for several reasons. These include:

1) the necessity of healing the mind of its belief that attack is salvation; this is accomplished through forgiveness, the undoing of our belief in the reality of separation and guilt.

2) emphasizing the importance of Jesus and/or the Holy Spirit as our loving and gentle Teacher, and developing a personal relationship with this Teacher.

3) correcting the errors of Christianity, particularly where it has emphasized suffering, sacrifice, separation, and sacrament as being inherent in God's plan for salvation.

Our thinking has always been inspired by Plato (and his mentor Socrates), both the man and his teachings. Plato's Academy was a place where serious and thoughtful people came to study his philosophy in an atmosphere conducive to their learning, and then returned to their professions to implement what they were taught by the great philosopher. Thus, by integrating abstract philosophical ideals with experience, Plato's school seemed to be the perfect model for the teaching center that we directed for so many years.

We therefore see the Foundation's principal purpose as being to help students of *A Course in Miracles* deepen their understanding of its thought system, conceptually and experientially, so that they may be more effective instruments of Jesus' teaching in their own lives. Since teaching forgiveness without experiencing it is empty, one of the Foundation's specific goals is to help facilitate the process whereby people may be better able to know that their own sins are forgiven and that they are truly loved by God. Thus is the Holy Spirit able to extend His Love through them to others.

Foundation for A Course in Miracles®
Temecula, California

Please see our Web site, www.facim.org, for a complete listing of publications and available translations. You may also write, or call our office for information:

Foundation for A Course in Miracles®
41397 Buecking Drive
Temecula, CA 92590
(951) 296-6261 • fax (951) 296-5455